Peter the Great & Catherine the Great: Russia's Greatest Tsar and Tsarina

By Charles River Editors

1698 portrait of Peter the Great

About Charles River Editors

Charles River Editors was founded by Harvard and MIT alumni to provide superior editing and original writing services, with the expertise to create digital content for publishers across a vast range of subject matter. In addition to providing original digital content for third party publishers, Charles River Editors republishes civilization's greatest literary works, bringing them to a new generation via ebooks.

Introduction

Peter the Great (1672-1725)

"I have conquered an empire, but have not been able to conquer myself." – Peter the Great

For anyone trying to understand the origins of modern Russia, the search should begin with Tsar Peter I (1672-1725), who titled himself Peter the Great during his lifetime. The moniker is fitting, considering the manner in which Peter brought Russia out of the Middle Ages and into the 18th century. Through a series of campaigns, Peter turned Russia into a formidable empire that would subsequently become a major force on the European continent, while also emulating Western Europe and turning Russia into an international state that interacted with the other continental powers. By revolutionizing and modernizing Russian arms, including the creation of Russia's first naval force, Peter was able to pursue an aggressive and expansionist foreign policy that set the stage for the way the European map would be redrawn again and again over the coming centuries. .

Perhaps more remarkably, as Peter was stretching Russia's borders, he was transforming Russia from the inside as well. Fond of the cultures to the west, Peter embraced technology, science and the arts, developing a new educational system for his people and supporting a number of institutions of higher learning in Russia. He built a European-style capital at St.

Petersburg and also established new ports and access to the Baltic Sea for the purposes of opening up trade with the west.

At the same time, if Peter was responsible for the modernization of Russia, he can also be held responsible for some of its more unsavory features. Though he accomplished a great many achievements during his reign, he also formally defined the status of Russian serfs for more than 200 years and bankrupted the Russian state with his navy, wars and building campaigns in St. Petersburg. Remedying the situations left by Peter would fall upon his successors, and not all of them would prove up to the challenges.

Peter the Great & Catherine the Great chronicles the life of the Russian Tsar and the profound historical legacy he left. Along with pictures of important people, places, and events, you will learn about Peter the Great like you never have before.

Catherine the Great (1729-1796)

"This princess seems to combine every kind of ambition in her person. Everything that may add luster to her reign will have some attraction for her. Science and the arts will be encouraged to flourish in the empire, projects useful for the domestic economy will be undertaken. She will endeavor to reform the administration of justice and to invigorate the laws; but her policies will be based on Machiavellianism; and I should not be surprised if in this field she rivals the king of Prussia. She will adopt the prejudices of her entourage regarding the superiority of her power and will endeavor to win respect not by the sincerity and probity of her actions but also by an ostentatious display of her strength. Haughty as she is, she will stubbornly pursue her undertakings and will rarely retrace a false step. Cunning and falsity appear to be vices in her character; woe to him who puts too much trust in her. Love affairs may become a stumbling block to her ambition and prove fatal for her peace of mind. This passionate princess, still held in check by the fear and consciousness of internal troubles, will know no restraint once she believes herself firmly established." - Baron de Breteuil

As one of the most famous women rulers in history, Russian Empress Catherine the Great has long been remembered not only as one of the most powerful women of her time, but she was also one of the most powerful and capable rulers in all of Europe. And her path to the throne was just as remarkable as her reign.

In a story that sounds like it could have been a precursor to Cinderella, Catherine the Great was born into a family of minor nobility, but she managed to forge her own destiny through her own cunning use of diplomacy and intrigue, gradually gaining allies and power. By 1762, she confident enough to conspire against her own husband, Peter III, whose reign as Tsar lasted just six months before his arrest at the hands of his wife. Upon his arrest and death, Catherine took power as the regent for their son, Grand Duke Paul.

Despite the strong-arm tactics, Catherine came to power in the midst of the Enlightenment, which was flourishing in France and Britain, and she would rule as an Enlightened ruler. A known correspondent of Voltaire's, Catherine sought to modernize Russia and turn it into a force in its own right, creating a rich and cultured court at the same time. Over the course of nearly 35 years in power, Catherine ushered in the Russian Enlightenment and presided over a period of time known as the Golden Age of the Russian Empire. Given her length of reign, forceful character, and lasting legacy, it was inevitable that legends about Catherine the Great would also pop up in the wake of her death. To an extent, certain legends have overshadowed her actual accomplishments, even as they continue to be circulated.

Peter the Great & Catherine the Great addresses the controversial legends about Catherine and her reign, but it also explores how a woman became one of the most powerful rulers in a country and continent dominated by men. Along with pictures of important people, places, and events, you will learn about Catherine the Great like you never have before.

Monument to Catherine in St. Petersburg

Peter the Great

Chapter 1: Peter's Early Years

Born in 1672, Peter was the son of Russian Tsar Alexis I and his second wife. Alexis I was a quiet, devout and somber man who fathered 13 children with his first wife, Maria Miloslavskaya. Of these children, only two sons survived their mother, making remarriage essential, so Tsar Alexis subsequently married Natalya Naryshkina, an intelligent and modest young woman, born into the lower nobility of Russia. Their marriage was a remarkably happy one, based on love, and they had two living children during their marriage: Peter and his younger sister Natalya.

Although Peter would later become incredibly tall and may have suffered from a form of epilepsy, he was born healthy and strong, and he was an active and intelligent young boy who divided his time between the Russian court at Moscow and the suburban summer palaces his mother favored. He lived a privileged life, surrounded by a staff of dwarves who served as his playmates.

Portrait of Peter as a child

At the time of his death in 1676, Alexis I was succeeded by Feodor III, Maria Miloslavskaya's oldest son. Feodor treated his stepmother and half-siblings well, and the remarkably well-educated (by Russian standards) tsar chose a tutor for Peter and oversaw his younger brother's education personally. He also encouraged Natalya and her children to remain at court, living comfortably in their apartments in the Kremlin.

Feodor III

Though Feodor married twice during his six-year reign, he did not produce a living heir so when he died in 1676, there were two potential heirs to the throne. His younger brother Ivan was 16, but Ivan was almost completely blind, physically disabled, and had a significant speech impediment. Conversely, 10 year old Peter was bright, healthy and so large for his age that when he was 12 years old, contemporaries thought they were looking at a 16 year old. Thus, after Feodor's death, the people of Moscow, gathered outside the Kremlin, chose Peter over Ivan, naming Natalya as his regent.

Though the people had chosen Natalya's son as Tsar, Natalya and her family did not have the support of the Streltsy, or Russian pikemen and musketeers, in Moscow. While there was not an ideal male heir to the throne among his two living sons, Alexis I had left behind a number of living daughters, but their lifestyles were not exactly conducive to taking power either. These Russian princesses lived on the upper floor of the palace completely isolated from men, and they left the palace heavily veiled only to attend church services. They would never marry, as foreign marriages were not acceptable and there was no one of equivalent rank available in Russia. Naturally, they were not well-educated and were only allowed to pray, gossip and work with the needles to pass the time.

However, one of Alexis' daughters, Sophia, was different. She was an active and educated member of the court, having persuaded her father to allow her unusual privileges from early childhood. Sophia, who was 19 when Tsar Alexis died, was bright, well-read and had been educated alongside her brother Feodor. She had also studied poetry, Polish, Latin, history and theology as a child.

During Feodor's reign, Sophia took an active role in the political life of the Russian court, participating in ruling councils of the nobility and acting as an advisor to her brother throughout his lifetime. When Feodor died, Sophia hoped for Ivan's coronation as the next in line for the throne, correctly surmising that since their mother was dead, Sophia herself would be made regent. Thus, she objected to Peter's election and made a very public display of her grief at Feodor's funeral, refusing to remain veiled or secluded. In response, Natalya removed Peter from the funeral, claiming he was unwell.

Sophia

On May 15, 1676, not long after Peter's election, the Streltsy in Moscow, still loyal to Maria Miloslavskaya's children, rose up against Peter and Natalya. They spread rumors that Feodor had been poisoned by the Naryshkins, and that Ivan had already been murdered to reduce any risk to Peter's right to inherit. While these rumors were not true, the heavily armed Streltsy marched on the Kremlin, posing a substantial threat to the royal family. Faced with a growing mob of angry and armed soldiers, Natalya calmly appeared before the mob with both Ivan and Peter, declaring both well and healthy. Her bravery and composure calmed the soldiers, but others in the court enraged them again by criticizing the Tsar and his mother loudly and publicly. In response, the Streltsy marched into the palace of the Kremlin, fighting the few available guards while the royal family hid. Many were killed during the conflict, including Natalya's brother, but eventually the fighting settled and calm returned to Moscow. The Streltsy demanded amnesty for their actions, backpay owed them by the crown, and even a triumphal column in the city square. All their demands were granted at once, even as the nobility began to tend to their dead.

About a week later, on May 23, the Streltsy suggested that Ivan be crowned co-Tsar along with Peter. Since Peter was already legally the Tsar, he could not be removed, but adding a second Tsar and replacing the regent was an acceptable alternative by Russian laws. The Patriarch of Moscow and the Russian nobility agreed to Ivan's coronation, even though the disabled young boy had no desire to rule and had to be convinced that he would have few actual duties. The Streltsy not only required Ivan's coronation but also specified a regent for the two boys, the Tsarevna Sophia. While there is no way to know if Sophia played a role in the uprising, the Miloslavskaya family certainly was involved in its planning and execution. Given her later successes and ambition, it seems likely that she was the author of this plot or at least a central figure within it

Peter and Ivan were required to sign documents and make occasional court appearances. However, Tsarevna Sophia took care of the day-to-day tasks of running Russia, with the assistance of her lover, Vasily Golitsyn. Regardless of his infirmities, Ivan did, as required by the state, marry and have several daughters. Still, there was little expectation that he would successfully produce a male heir. By then, Peter was already the crowned co-Tsar, reducing the need for an heir.

Vasily Golitsyn

Tsarevna Sophia ruled for seven years, from 1682-1689, and those who doubted her abilities to rule were greatly mistaken. Though her heavy hand ensured peace, it also left Russian society in the same stable (and backwards) condition she found it, and when she was forced to go to war against the Crimean Tatars, she was unsuccessful. Still, her lover Golitsyn, as head of the Russian army, re-entered Moscow feigning victory in September 1687, a gimmick he would attempt during subsequent losses the following spring. Sophia's attempt to falsify Russia's military success backfired, however, weakening her claim to the throne.

Sophia paid little attention to either Peter or his mother after her regency began in 1682, but she provided Natalya with a small allowance and allowed her and Peter to live outside the city of Moscow. Thus, Peter grew up in the countryside at Preobrazhenskoe, which had been a favorite countryside retreat for Alexis I. There, without the support of his brother Feodor, Peter abandoned his formal education and immersed himself in military drills and war games, using his playmates as soldiers.

By Peter's early teens, some 300 young men lived in barracks at Preobrazhenskoe, and a second group of 300 resided in a nearby village. Ultimately, these two groups would become the first and second regiment of the Russian Imperial Guard, founded by Peter himself to replace the less disciplined Streltsy. In regular letters to Sophia, Peter made frequent requests for military gear and supplies from the state armories, and Sophia granted these without question. Additional facilities were built at Preobrazhenskoe to house and train the force of 600, and western-style uniforms were made to replace Russian uniforms.

Peter even enlisted himself in his guard at the lowest levels, first as a drummer boy, and he worked his way up through the ranks as noblemen in his army would later be required to do. During his teens, he was particularly partial to working as an artilleryman, enjoying both the technology of war and the lively noise. As his war games grew along with him, he hired experienced foreign officers to help teach and plan siege warfare strategies and more complex mock campaigns.

While Peter was especially fond of military play, he was also a remarkably curious young man, During these years at Preobrazhenskoe, he mastered a variety of skills, including crafts of all sorts. He learned carpentry, masonry, smithing and printing from local craftsmen, and he would also work alongside them throughout his life. In 1688, while accompanied by a European friend, Peter saw his first European boat, a small English sailing ship that had been given to Tsar Alexis and stored in a nearby barn. Enthralled by the boat, so different than the shallow-bottomed river going vessels of Russia, he had it repaired by European shipwrights and learned to sail it himself. As his love for water grew, Peter built his first shipyard at a nearby lake. He did not just fund the shipyard but also lived in a simple cottage and worked alongside the builders from dawn until dusk.

In 1688, Natalya decided that marriage might settle Peter down, encourage him to remain at home, and turn his attention toward political activity and producing an heir. With Peter's agreement, she chose a quiet, devout and submissive young woman, Eudoxia Lopukhina, from among the Russian nobility, but the marriage was not a success for the ill-matched couple. Peter found Eudoxia both unintelligent and uninteresting, and he actively resented the young woman. They had two sons in two years, but only one, Alexei, survived infancy. Once he had provided the required heir, Peter ignored his bride and spent his time with European friends at Preobrazhenskoe and elsewhere.

As a young man, Peter's appearance was rather remarkable. He stood more than six and a half feet tall, a giant by 17th century standards, but he was also thin and angular rather than muscular, despite years of physical labor. He avoided wigs, keeping his own hair only moderately long, and he also preferred comfortable and well-worn clothing over royal regalia. After contracting a high fever in 1693, he developed a visible facial tic or tremor that may have been a mild form of epilepsy, and it made him both self-conscious and shy. An Italian visitor to his court would later describe Peter: "Tsar Peter was tall and thin, rather than stout. His hair was thick, short, and dark brown; he had large eyes, black with long lashes, a well-shaped mouth, but the lower lip was slightly disfigured ... For his great height, his feet seemed very narrow. His head was sometimes tugged to the right by convulsions."

Chapter 2: Becoming a Man

While Ivan posed no threat to Sophia's reign, Peter certainly did, because once he came of age there would be no justification for Sophia to continue ruling as regent.

Following the failed Crimean campaign in 1688, Sophia's position with both the military and the people of Russia was less secure, and tension between she and Peter continued to grow. Still, neither one of them initially decided to make a move. Peter commanded only 600 men and was not yet prepared to take control of the state by force, while Sophia refused to act on the advice of advisers who advocated having Peter killed before he could come to power. .

On August 17, 1689, Sophia ordered a large company of Streltsy to accompany her on a pilgrimage to a nearby monastery. However, when she received news that Peter was considering an attempt on her life, she summoned additional guards. During the course of the day, more rumors circulated through the Kremlin, causing her to summon even more guards and order the gates of the Kremlin closed. When a routine messenger arrived from Peter's home in Preobrazhenskoe, he was badly beaten by Sophia's guards. Suspicious because of the troop build-up and closed gates, Peter's men feared an attempt on his life. That night, a rider reached Peter and warned him that he was in danger. Peter fled from his bed into the woods and left at once for the fortified Troitsky monastery some miles away. While Sophia had not planned an attempt on his life, Peter's rushed trip to Troitsky marked the turning point in his youth and his reign.

From the fortified monastery, Peter consolidated power and began to act as Tsar of Russia in his own right for the first time. He ordered each of the commanders of the Streltsy to come to his side and bring a few of his best men. Faced with her own demise, Sophia attempted to reconcile with Peter in the following days, offering to rule alongside him, but Peter rebuffed her attempts and soon gained the support of the Patriarch in Moscow and the remainder of the Russian military. By September 11, 1689, Sophia had only a few allies remaining. Peter ordered her to leave the Kremlin and go to a convent, where she would spend the rest of her life.

On October 16, 1689, 17 year old Peter entered the Kremlin victorious and formally claimed his position, though he was still only officially co-Tsar alongside Ivan. Peter soon returned to Preobrazhenskoe and his usual life, while the everyday work of governing was done by a small group, including Natalya, for the next five years. However, Natalya lacked Sophia's strength or intelligence, and while the council administered affairs the Russian government was chaotic and corrupt. Throughout the first few years of his adult reign, Peter took no real interest in the work of governing, even when he objected to the council's actions.

From 1690 onward, Peter spent a great deal of time in the German Suburb, a western enclave close to Preobrazhenskoe. Foreigners had been expelled from the city of Moscow and required to live in their own district a few years earlier, and various soldiers, merchants and engineers all lived in the European-style neighborhood with their wives and families. There, among the wide streets, formal gardens, afternoon tea and evening salons, Peter drank, smoked and talked about politics, art, and warfare through the night. As he gradually fit in better, Peter was invited to parties, weddings, and baptisms, often giving away the bride or serving as godfather to newly baptized infants.

During these days in the European neighborhood, Peter became close to two important men, Scottish General Patrick Gordon and Swiss adventurer Francis Lefort. Gordon would tutor Peter in military strategy, while Lefort would provide Peter with companionship and support for many years. A large group gathered around the young Tsar, with 80-200 people gathering regularly for large banquets hosted by Lefort in a generous mansion paid for and provided by Peter, and members of Peter's large entourage, called the Jolly Company, frequently met there even when Peter himself was not available. His friends all had nicknames, often in direct defiance of any sort of court protocol. One was even assigned the title of King of Pressburg and addressed as "Your Majesty" by Peter himself.

To say the young men lived a debaucherous lifestyle would be an understatement, as contemporary writers noted that "they consumed gargantuan portions of food and drink, leaving the table to play ninepins, or bowls, or for archery matches and musket practice, then returning to eat again. More often than not these banquets degenerated into debauchery and drunkenness on a grand scale"

While Peter had not enjoyed his wife's company, he did like the European women he met in the German Suburb, who were nothing like the Russian women he had known growing up. During these years, he became involved with the daughter of a Dutch wine merchant, Anna Mons, remaining close for several years. Mons clearly hoped to marry Peter after he divorced Eudoxia, but she would have to settle for being his semi-official royal mistress from 1691-1703.

During these years, Peter continued to play war games with his 600 soldiers and to spend time building his boats at Lake Pleschev, staying away from Moscow for months at a time. In 1693, Peter planned a visit to Russia's only port, Archangel, located upriver from the White Sea, and he had a small yacht, the St. Peter, built for his use. While he sailed to the edge of the White Sea, Peter did not venture into open waters, having promised his mother he would not risk his life, but when he returned to Archangel after his mother's death in the spring of 1694, he sailed from the river through the White Sea. In one letter home around this time, Peter wrote of his celebratory mood after the creation of a man-of-war: "What I have long wished is now being realized. You shall hear more by next post. Now to make merry. It is difficult to write in detail, or rather, it is impossible. On such occasions when one reverences Bacchus, who with his vine-leaves covers up the eyes of those who want to write long letters."

Ivan, who had played so little role in the state administration, died in February 1696, leaving a widow and three daughters, but, more importantly, his death required Peter to take a more active role in the running of the state. While the two men had spent little time together, Peter had always been kind to Ivan and was apparently fond enough of him to continue caring for Ivan's widow and three daughters after his death, eventually ensuring that they were married to European nobles.

Peter was now the sole Tsar of Russia, and for the first time he fully accepted his adult responsibilities.

Chapter 3: The Traveling Tsar

Even before he took the reins of power by himself, Peter had started trying to put his military training to use. In 1695, he initiated a military offensive against the Crimean Tatars and the port city of Azov, but his siege failed when his troops were unable to encircle the port city without a navy. Peter lost a number of men and was forced to withdraw his forces that Fall, but he hadn't given up his ambitions. That winter, he ordered the construction of a new shipyard and constructed a fleet of vessels to attack Azov by sea rather than by land. Peter himself joined in the work, putting many hours of work in each day as a carpenter on the ships.

Peter's new naval force and renewed dedication paid dividends in the summer of 1696 when he successfully forced the surrender of Azov. He now had access to a port on the Sea of Azov, but he did not yet have the right to travel and trade throughout the Black Sea. This limited the usefulness of his conquest by preventing him from establishing the trade routes he wanted.

Illustration depicting Peter capturing Azov

At the same time, the success in Azov immediately sparked Peter's desire for a larger and more effective naval force. The government, nobility, merchants and church were all required to commit funds to create a navy for the Russian state, which led to increased criticisms of Peter's naval projects, but Peter was able to quell dissatisfaction. At his request, shipbuilders from Venice, Holland and elsewhere came to Russia to help build galleys, and in conjunction with that Peter sent a number of Russians west to learn about sailing, shipbuilding and navigation from experienced builders and sailors in Europe.

Shortly thereafter, Peter's government announced plans for a large expedition west, called the Grand Embassy, which consisted of more than 250 soldiers, ambassadors and nobles, including a well-disguised Peter traveling incognito. While not officially acknowledged, Peter was typically received by the other monarchs during this journey, and other times he was simply present when Francis Lefort, the chief ambassador, met the kings of western Europe. A regency council governed during Peter's absence, and on his journey, Tsar Peter I met with Frederick I of Prussia, the Electresses of Hanover and Brandenburg, and others. Though temperamental, he made a relatively good impression on the other rulers, who remembered both his manners and courtesy. However, his clandestine attempt to form an alliance against the Ottoman Turks received a lukewarm response on his tour of Europe.

Frederick I of Prussia

After his return to Russia, Peter sent a number of unusually tall men to Frederick I for Frederick's collection of exceptionally tall soldiers, known as the Potsdam Giants. These human collections were popular among both Russian and western nobles, and Frederick became notorious for using his own army like living toy soldiers. After visiting Prussia, Peter went on to Holland, the most economically successful of the European states, to learn both shipbuilding and more about Holland's successful trade empire. Meeting an old friend there, Peter settled into a modest wooden house and found work at a shipyard. Rumors soon spread through Zaandam that the Tsar was visiting, and though he had hoped to spend several months in the town, once his identity was discovered he only remained for one week.

Nevertheless, Peter went on to spend several months in Amsterdam, again working as a carpenter and even cooking his own meals. He sent his men throughout Holland to learn carpentry, shipbuilding and artillery skills, while Peter himself visited mills, laboratories and even observed several surgical dissections. Peter enjoyed his visit to Holland but realized he needed to learn more about shipbuilding than he had learned in Holland.

Statue of Peter the Great doing shipbuilding in the city of Saardam, Holland

With the permission of William of Orange, the King of England, Peter next planned a trip to England to see the large-scale shipbuilding operations that provided England with the best navy in Europe. Once again the studying was hands-on, as Peter worked at the dockyards and visited mints and printing presses located in the Tower of London. Peter remained in England until May 1698, but his visit was not entirely successful; the English court was quite glad to see both Peter and his rowdy men go. The damage they did was extensive, according to at least one account: "Some notion of the boisterous high jinks that took place may be obtained from considering the damage done. They broke three hundred panes of glass. They had bust or prised open the brass locks of twelve doors. They had blown up the kitchen floor...they cut up the dressers and several doors. They covered the parlour floor with grease and ink; broke walnut tables and stands. They seem to have had wild games in the beds, tearing up the feather beds, ripping the sheets, tearing canopies to pieces and ruining precious silk counterpanes." As one of his biographers put it, "The young Tsar had a strong head and an iron constitution. All-night drinking bouts became one of his regular diversions and, while others were deep in drunken slumber after a night's orgy, he would rise at down to work...it did not abate the tremendous energy that erupted from him, nor did it prevent his doing the work of ten men throughout his life. For him, heavy drinking was a form of relaxation from his labours, releasing the great pressure of physical and nervous energy...[it] did not leave him debauched or incapable, bt refreshed him for the next day's work"

Peter's travels may have suggested that he was more interested in boyish pursuits than being Tsar, but despite his distance from Russia, Peter received regular letters and became more and more interested in the affairs of state than he had been before. This was particularly the case when challenges to his rule popped up, like in July 1698, when Peter learned of a possible Streltsy uprising in Russia. Peter canceled the remainder of his journey to return to Moscow, but he traveled through Poland along the way and met the Polish King Augustus, taking time out to formulate an expanding plan of attack against Sweden with the Polish king. While dealing with internal enemies, it was apparent that Peter was also envisioning a larger and more powerful Russian state.

When Peter reached Moscow on September 4, 1698, he went about immediately putting down the Streltsy revolt, after which he began to institute substantial internal changes to the laws and customs of the Russian people.

Chapter 4: Peter the Visionary

Peter's Grand Embassy had helped him learn more about various nations across Europe, but he also brought more than 800 European employees back to Russia as well. And though his somewhat eccentric behavior puzzled many, the European courts now recognized a possible powerful ally in the Russian monarch.

For Russia itself, Peter took home several lessons from his travels. Attributing European success to the Renaissance and Reformation, Peter believed he needed to weaken the Orthodox Church in Russia and create a more secular state, so in 1700 he began to take control of both the management of the Church and its incomes. He had never been particularly devout, and though he embraced some aspects of change he had seen in the West, he had no interest in constitutional monarchies, parliaments, or other means of sharing his own absolute power as Tsar.

Furthermore, shortly after his return Peter forced the Russians to accept the dress and customs he had seen in the West. The problem with this step was that the old-fashioned Russian clothes and the traditional heavy beard may were intentionally well-designed to manage the cold winters. Heavy clothing and hair reduced the risk of frostbite on the face and appendages. The Russian people also tied their appearance to their religious beliefs. When men were ordered to shave their beards, it caused them significant spiritual and personal distress because the unshaven and untrimmed beard had long been a symbol of faith for Russian Orthodox adult males. Peter himself shaved the men in his own circle, often taking a good bit of skin along with the hair. Sensing the changing times, cautious and ambitious men alike opted to shave before meeting with Peter in order to curry his favor, and even within his Jolly Company, only a few elderly men were spared the new regulation. Meanwhile, a tax allowed men in the general population to keep their beards, but it was quite costly.

Western dress soon replaced the heavy Russian attire, at least in Moscow, and soon became the law of the land. Long, heavy Russian coats were to be replaced by a waistcoat, breeches and hat, rather than a fur-trimmed hood. Women were to wear petticoats, skirts and bonnets instead of the long, loose, brightly colored robes that were traditional. Corsets, unknown in Russia, were also introduced. While men resisted these changes, women embraced the new fashions, ordering clothing from Paris and requesting fashion drawings to have their own dressmakers reproduce stylish garments.

European-style architecture, gardens and other aspects of life also became stylish in Russia, with wealthy Russians being encouraged to embrace tea parties and European-style social galas. Peter shocked his own court by welcoming Russian noblewomen at social gatherings, creating a new place for wives and daughters within the lives and social circles of the nobility. Ironically, one of the women who did not care for these changes was Peter's wife Eudoxia, who was a very traditional Russian woman. While he was still traveling in Europe, he wrote home encouraging his council to suggest Eudoxia become a nun, but she refused because she didn't want to be separated from her son. Peter crafted a solution to this nettlesome issue by simply forcing her into a convent, an act that ended his troubled marriage. Once Eudoxia entered a convent, he was considered divorced and free to remarry, while their living son, Alexei, was placed into the care of his sister Natalya. Eudoxia remained in a convent or imprisoned in a fortress until her grandson, Peter II, came to power many years later.

While some of the changes upon Peter's return were superficial, others were more significant. For example, Peter instituted a new calendar in line with that of Western Europe to allow improved communication with the West. Today the Orthodox calendar remains different from the one used by the different Christian branches in Western Europe, but in Peter's time they were all on the same schedule.

Influenced by his visit to the mint in London, Peter also ordered the production of new, government-regulated coinage to stabilize the economy. Taking an anonymous suggestion from a serf (whom he later found and freed), Peter had specially printed paper created for government documents. Trade monopolies helped to fund the government treasury, beginning with a tobacco deal Peter negotiated while in London. Though tobacco had been condemned by the Orthodox Church, it was embraced by Peter's court, like so many other European customs. Additional monopolies followed, enabling the government to make significant profits as the desire for European goods grew.

In addition to strengthening the Russian economy, Peter also went about fortifying Russia and the burgeoning empire he was already envisioning. Peter's failed military expedition at Azov, his military experience with his own regiments, and his own observations had all proven to him that the Streltsy were poorly trained and inadequate for achieving his goals. In fact, following the engagements at Azov, Peter had left most of the Streltsy in border areas, instead relying upon his own guard within the city. Naturally, the Streltsy resented the changes in the military under Peter's rule and began to complain about poor or absent wages in the border areas of Russia, but their revolt during Peter's Grand Embassy only drove home his point. While Peter was in Western Europe, a large group of Streltsy gathered and began to march through Russia, moving into the central region of the country from the area around Azov. But once they marched toward Moscow, the Streltsy were met by General Gordon and the Imperial Guard, who brought the revolt under control and quickly secured their surrender. Gordon captured more than 1,500 Streltsy and led them to Moscow in chains. Large facilities were quickly created to manage the mass torture and eventual execution of most of the prisoners, and tortured Streltsy admitted to a plan to remove the Tsar, burn the German Suburb and gain control of the city. They intended to place Sophia in power, offering the throne to Peter's son Alexei if she refused. If Alexei refused, one of Sophia's former advisors would become Tsar. As a result, several of Sophia's attendants in the convent were also whipped and executed, despite there being no evidence of guilt. Peter only spared those who offered information freely, believing that widespread torture and execution would maintain discipline and prevent further rebellion.

Mass executions followed the Streltsy revolt, ranging from relatively merciful hangings and beheadings to public dismemberment, breaking on the wheel, burning alive and other brutal public means of execution. Many of the bodies were conspicuously displayed near the convent where Sophia and Peter's wife Eudoxia lived. After the Streltsy uprising, Sophia was forced to shave her head and take permanent vows at the convent, taking the name Susannah. She was no longer allowed visitors, and her movements were limited, even within the convent. One of her sisters was also forced to take vows, eliminating the possibility that she could become involved in a rebellion.

Ilya Repin's painting depicting Sophia in a cell within the Novodevichy Convent, with one of the Streltsy visibly hanging outside her window.

Chapter 5: Peter the Husband

After ending his arranged marriage to Eudoxia, Peter chose his second wife, Catherine, for love. Born Marta Helena Skowrońska, she had been raised by a Polish-Lithuanian Lutheran minister named Johann Ernst Gluck. No attempt was made to educate her, even in that highly literate household, and she remained illiterate throughout her life. Captured as a prisoner of war in her teens, she was placed into the household of Field Marshal Boris Sheremetev, where she converted to the Orthodox faith, taking the name Catherine. By 1703, when she met Peter, she was living in the household of Peter's advisor and close friend, Alexander Menshikov, who may have purchased the 17-year-old girl.

Catherine I

Catherine's role in Menshikov's home is unclear, but she was high-ranking enough to speak to the Tsar and attend or serve at a function attended by royalty. Catherine had a curvaceous figure, thick blond hair and black eyes, making her an appealing young woman even if she was not beautiful by upper-class standards. More important than Catherine's appearance for Peter was her disposition; she was warm, loving, honest and kind, providing Peter with unconditional love. He began an affair with her at once, but she remained in the Menshikov household during this time, other than when she and Menshikov's mistress, Darya, were traveling together to the army camps with their lovers. The quartet was happiest when they were all together, whether at home or on the battlefield.

In 1706, at Peter's insistence, Menshikov married Darya, while Peter and Catherine were secretly married in November 1707. The marriage remained a secret until 1711, when Peter told his sister and sister-in-law that Catherine was now his wife and should be treated as his widow if he died. Catherine and Peter were thus publicly married in a lavish ceremony in 1712, formalizing their relationship.

Unlike Eudoxia, Catherine did not remain at home while Peter was at war, instead deciding to travel with him. This made her an integral part of his day-to-day life, and not surprisingly she was one of the few who could calm and soothe him when he had an epileptic seizure or became upset. When they were apart, they wrote each other often, sending small gifts with each letter, as indicated by one of Peter's letters to her from Berlin in October 1712: "Yesterday I arrived here and I went to see the King. Yesterday morning, he came to me and last night I went to the Queen. I send you as many oysters as I could find. I couldn't get any more because they say the plague has broken out in Hamburg and it is forbidden to bring anything from there."

Early in their relationship, Catherine lived with their children and Peter in the simple wooden cabin in St. Petersburg, caring for her family as the women of the working classes did. When Peter moved from the cabin to a palace, so did Catherine, adapting to both his desire to live simply and to the banquets and formalities of court. While she had been raised a peasant, Catherine learned to dance in court and enjoyed both fine clothing and jewels. In this endeavor she was assisted by the fact that Peter maintained an informal court, frequently dining alone with Catherine. Even when he dined with his ministers, the servants were dismissed when dessert was served to allow them to speak privately. Peter favored simple foods, including soups, stews, fruit and dark bread at his meals, eating these foods even when richer ones were served at the table. He wore old clothes, with stockings mended by his wife and daughters.

In 1704, Catherine bore a son named Peter, and he was followed by a new child nearly each year thereafter for a total of twelve children. Unfortunately, ten of these died in infancy or early childhood, and only one of their children, Elizabeth, lived long enough to marry. These repeated losses were devastating for both Peter and Catherine, particularly the loss of their last son, Peter, in 1721.

Chapter 6: Peter the Empire Builder

Peter always hoped to make Russia into a naval power and create the kind of trade empire that he had studied and visited in the West, but he could not do this without access to high-quality, accessible ports for trade. During his Great Embassy, he began to consider retaking lands along the Baltic Sea, which had been lost to Sweden in 1613, and creating port cities that could provide access to open waters, enable trade between Russia and Europe, and increase the possibility for travel by sea.

Russia had several allies in this fight, including Poland-Lithuania and Denmark. Sweden's king, Charles XII, was quite young and untested in war, and both Russia and its allies expected an easy victory with relatively limited losses. They began the war with an unprovoked attack against Swedish territories at three different locations, only for the Swedes to make significant gains at once. It was soon clear that this would not be a short or simple war.

Charles XII of Sweden

By August 1700, Charles XII had succeeded in making peace with Denmark, and that November Charles XII and Peter I met in battle for the first time. Peter besieged the city of Narva, setting up encampments with a force of 35,000 men, while Charles, with a force of only 8,000, marched toward Narva, encountering only small detachments of Russian troops along the way. Peter personally left Narva as Charles and his army approached, believing that the Russian troops were well-placed in secure entrenchments around the city and would be victorious. Instead, Charles' army of 8,000 attacked the Russians during a blizzard and the Russian army collapsed under the attack; 20,000 Russian infantrymen were taken prisoner and forced to surrender their muskets before being released. Russian losses may have numbered as many as 10,000 men killed in battle; with many more drowning while attempting to flee. The Swedes lost only 600 soldiers during the attack, preserving most of Charles XII's army and increasing morale among his Swedish troops.

Peter used his loss at Narva as a propaganda tool, claiming that the poor training and discipline in the army led to the Swedish victory. Thus, he encouraged the nobility to support his attempt to change the military structure of Russia, and by the end of 1701 Peter had begun to formulate a plan to redesign his army, add an additional imperial fleet, and improve his chances for military success. This began when he founded the School of Mathematics and Navigation to train the skilled navigators his fleet would require, along with a similar school to provide training in artillery and weaponry for the army. Shipbuilding began around 1702, with a number of ships complete and ready for use by 1703. By 1724, the Russian imperial fleet included 141 sail-driven warships and many more oar-driven ships.

Eventually Charles pulled his forces back, and this retreat allowed the Russians to gain significant ground along the Baltic Sea. In 1702, the Russians took the fortress at Noteburg (modern-day Oreshek), and in 1703 they took the fortress of Nienchanz. Peter immediately began to build up these newly conquered lands, including creating the new capital city of St. Petersburg near the former fortress of Nienchan. Peter attacked Narva again, as well as Dorpat, in 1704, and this time he was far more successful. Dorpat fell quickly and Narva followed with ease, after which the Swedes still unfortunate enough to be there were butchered by Russian troops. Several months later, Peter returned to Moscow, celebrating his victory. His earlier loss at Narva was redeemed, and much of the Baltic was secured.

Nikolay Sauerweid's painting depicts Peter stopping some of his marauding soldiers after

they captured Narva in 1704

Leaving a portion of his army behind to secure the throne of Poland, Charles began to march east toward Russia in 1706, planning to proceed directly to Moscow rather than trying to take back conquered lands along the Baltic coast. Peter made preparations for battle by sending troops into Western Poland to destroy the countryside and eliminate access to food for Swedish troops. He also expanded his own army and fortified the city of Moscow. Having lost his throne to Charles, the king of Poland, Augustus II, also made his way to Russia, serving as a commander under Peter.

Before reaching Moscow, Charles attacked the fortress of Grodno, but the Russian troops managed to hold out in the fortress, despite the fact a second detachment of Russians, Poles and Saxons was defeated on their way to defend Grodno and help those trapped in the fortress under siege. Eventually the defenders managed to escape early that spring, after nearly starving over the winter.

The siege of Grodno destroyed towns and villages in the surrounding area before Charles left Russian soil in the summer. The Swedes were unopposed in Saxony, and the Saxon nobles signed a peace treaty without Augustus's support, leaving the Polish ruler in the difficult position of having lost power in both Poland and Saxony. With Poland out of the war for good, Peter was alone and without allies. While he considered peace negotiations, Charles rejected his offers and refused to consider anything but a full surrender.

Charles planned an attack on Russia once again after his brief retreat into Saxony, but this time he found the Russian troops were better trained and organized than they had been several years earlier. Meanwhile, many battles, poor conditions, limited food and dysentery had damaged his own army, reducing both its strength and morale. Charles finally marched south into the Ukraine, looking for adequate food and new Cossack soldiers. He had been communicating with the head of the Cossacks, Mazeppa, who had once defected to Sweden, but the majority of the Cossacks themselves remained loyal to the Tsar.

As so many other rulers would learn, the Russian Winter was the greatest enemy their troops could face. The winter of 1708, spent in the harsh Ukraine, decimated the Swedish troops, with thousands dying from the cold and illness. Charles himself was wounded in a skirmish that winter, and as he lay ill, the Russians defeated the Swedes at the Battle of Poltava in 1709. Charles attended the battle on a stretcher, but he was unable to either fight or command. When the battle ended, the remnants of the Swedish army retreated toward the south as Charles XII took a small force and prepared to enter Ottoman territory and request sanctuary under the direct protection of the Sultan.

The Swedes had lost more than half of their army at Poltava, with nearly 7,000 dead or wounded and another 2,760 captured. While Swedish casualties were high, Peter's army had fewer than 5,000 total casualties and only 1,345 deaths in the battle. On July 1, the remainder of the Swedish army surrendered to Peter, while their king was already safely in Ottoman territory. The Swedes were well-treated, but the Cossacks under Swedish command were treated as traitors and executed. Peter even allowed Swedish officers to enlist in the Russian army and retain their ranks, and many subsequently learned trades or became teachers in Peter's newly created school system. Some even entered Peter's administration as government bureaucrats. Common soldiers in the Swedish army had fewer options, but they could still serve in the Russian army or work as laborers.

Mikhail Lomonosov's mosaic depicting Peter at the Battle of Poltava

Following the victory at Poltava, kings throughout Europe moved to create alliances with Peter, recognizing the changing status of Russia. He reestablished his alliances with both Denmark and Poland, now once again in Augustus II's hands, and Peter negotiated with King Frederick I of Prussia during the months after Poltava to create a valuable European alliance. He also arranged two foreign marriages during this time, marrying his son to a foreign princess and one of his nieces to a foreign prince.

In 1710, with the encouragement of Charles XII and his remaining allies, the Ottoman Empire declared war on Russia. The peace treaty between the two countries, the 1700 Treaty of Constantinople (which had been negotiated by Peter after the conquest of Azov), had lasted for just 10 years, but that time had allowed Peter to focus on a single enemy at a time. At the Swedish king's urging, the Ottomans prepared to march north from Crimea into the Russian

Ukraine, but this time Charles refused to join their army, perhaps fearful of what might await him there.

While Peter had not chosen to go to war with the Turks, his army was strong, well-prepared and confident after the victory at Poltava, and on February 25, 1711, Peter proclaimed a holy war "against the enemies of Christ". Peter planned to counter the Turkish attack by threatening Adrianople, hoping that a relatively small force would receive aid from the Christian people of the region, including Walachia and Moldavia. Russian propaganda presented Peter as the liberator of Balkan Christians, both Catholic and Orthodox, but Peter was unprepared to face the kind of army led by the Grand Vizier of the Ottoman Empire. The Turkish leader had some 200,000 men under his command, and Peter did not receive the hoped-for support from Christians in Walachia. By July of 1712, the meeting of the two armies could no longer be avoided, and the Turkish army outnumbered Peter's hungry, exhausted and sickly force by more than five times its number.

While outnumbered, the Russians inflicted substantial damage on the Turkish Janissaries, and though the Russians ultimately lost the battle, the Turks were uninterested in engaging in another full-scale battle. Peter offered terms of surrender and sent word that the Russians would accept nearly any terms, but to their pleasant surprise the Grand Vizier offered Peter relatively favorable terms. He would lose lands gained in 1696 and 1700, including Azov, Russian troops had to leave Poland and grant Charles XII passage home over land, and Peter had to try to make peace with Charles. There were also rumors that Catherine and the other women at the camp had promised the Grand Vizier their jewels in exchange for Peter's safety.

The Grand Vizier was pleased with his success, but the Sultan and Charles XII were both less so. The Treaty at Pruth ended the war between Russia and the Turks, but it did not lead to peace between the two powers, and Peter avoided surrendering the southern cities until April 1712. With this surrender, Peter's hope for southern expansion also ended. Meanwhile, Charles XII attempted to initiate hostilities between the Turks and Russians repeatedly over the coming years, resulting in several short conflicts, but by 1713, the Turks were weary of his interference and hoped for a lasting peace with Russia. That January, the Sultan ordered Charles XII abducted and put onto a French ship bound for Sweden. Charles resisted violently, and after several days of fighting he was escorted to Adrianople, where he spent several weeks recovering from his injuries. Though he agreed to leave the Ottoman Empire willingly on a French ship; instead, he eventually made the journey by land, maintaining a remarkable pace on his return home and finally reaching Swedish soil for the first time in years in November 1714. Charles remained in Swedish Pomerania until an attack by Danish and Prussian forces compelled him to escape to Sweden on the night of Christmas Eve, 1715.

Though Peter's hopes of expansion had been blunted in the south by the Ottomans, he made significant territorial gains elsewhere. By 1718 the Russians had conquered most of Finland, the port of Riga, and the Swedish city of Vyborg. These gains in the Baltic Sea strengthened the burgeoning Russian empire and provided ports and access to the rich resources of Finland, including valuable meat and lumber. Peter also proved to be a rather benevolent conqueror, allowing these regions to maintain both their faith and culture.

With his naval forces strengthened and experienced in battle, Peter commenced an invasion of Sweden in 1720. Peter's newly-built and well-designed galleys could navigate both open water and shallow rivers, making them ideal for battle in the region of the Baltic Sea. Charles XII, having returned to Sweden not long before, did not survive the war, dying in Norway in November 1718. With the death of Charles, Sweden sued for peace, and eventually Peter signed the Treaty of Nistadt in 1721, ending the war between Russia and Sweden. Peter and Russia retained their gains in the Baltic, including the newly founded capital city of St. Petersburg (built at the site of the 1703 victory at Nienchanz), and secured very favorable terms.

After the treaty, the Russian Senate named Peter Emperor of Russia, the first to be called by that title.

Chapter 7: Peter the Great

While Peter was rarely in the Russian capital of Moscow before St. Petersburg was built and often remained away from the state capital even after its construction, he continued to make laws and order new taxes with a tight grip on power. Perhaps due to the fact that he was constantly away from Moscow, in 1708 he attempted to decentralize the government by creating eight individual districts, but it would not prove successful. In 1711, Peter created the Russian Senate to approve laws and govern when he was away at war or otherwise unavailable, and since his efforts at war required a huge amount of money and a large number of men, he expected the Senate was to provide them in his absence. However, the establishment of the Russian Senate was anything but smooth, and new rules had to be passed in 1715 and 1720 simply to improve order in the chaotic Senate. The men were often neglectful in their duties and belligerent to each other, forcing Peter to create a system of colleges (or ministries) that would handle government affairs in 1718. He based these on a Western European model, in which the college presidents were made members of the Senate, and foreigners also could serve in the colleges. In 1722, Peter continued to tinker with the structure of government by creating the office of Procurator General, which was intended to provide an imperial voice and supervision within the Senate.

Even with substantial new taxes and trade monopolies, the government struggled with mounting debt, and the taxes and labor conscription were unpopular. To pacify his people, Peter established other measures to improve conditions for the people of Russia. Peter included women in society and forbade the practice of arranged marriages; newborn children with deformities were not to be smothered at birth; and similar protections were extended to illegitimate children. New penalties punished those who killed unwanted infants throughout Russia, and Russian emperors and empresses would subsequently start taking an interest in neglected or unwanted children.

In addition to trying to establish some semblance of order in the Russian Senate, Peter banned men from wearing daggers and knives, reducing the risk of death in street fights. He also created the first public hospital in Russia to provide care to the people of St. Petersburg, while also guaranteeing that foreigners became a protected class by giving them additional freedoms that would also conveniently encourage skilled workers to migrate to Russia.

Peter also modernized Russia's educational system. For the first time, education became a civic duty and a requirement for the nobility, and it was also encouraged in the middle classes. From the ages of 10-15, young noble boys were enrolled in compulsory education, and though Peter's attempts to extend compulsory education to the middle class failed, educational opportunities improved with the founding of several specialized schools and the increased printing of books in Russia.

After completing their educations at the age of 15, the nobility would begin careers by entering 25 years of required government service, starting as a private in the lowest levels of the military and working their way up through the ranks. At the same time, merit-based promotion meant that men from lower levels of society could also gain status, and no more than one-third of the members of a single family could serve in the civil service instead of the military, further evening the playing field. Peter attempted to establish new inheritance laws that eliminated the rights of the oldest son and allowed inheritance by merit, but the law was eventually abolished in response to the great deal of unrest it caused.

While Peter instituted a number of reforms, he also implemented and formalized traditional Russian notions of class and service. In many ways, serfdom was quite similar to chattel slavery in Europe and the United States during the 18th and 19th centuries. Serfs could be bought or sold without regard to family ties, and they could be whipped or beaten as punishment. While they could not be executed, they could be punished to the point of death. And any child born to parents who were serfs was, by definition, already tied to the land and a part of the property on which he or she was born.

In Peter's time, as many as 95 percent of the population were serfs, and he created new taxes, based on the "soul tax" he had seen in France, that further tied the serfs to the land and made it impossible for the serfs to legally leave the land they were born on. The state, the crown and the nobility owned serfs, and later the merchant classes were allowed to own serfs as well. In the same vein, near the end of his reign Peter transformed the household slaves of the Russian nobility into house serfs, giving them the same legal standing as the agricultural serfs of Russia. In order to meet a growing need for industrial labor and miners, Peter decreed that factories could own serfs, and that agricultural serfs who fled for the factories were not to be pursued, but simply allowed to become factory workers.

Peter's control of the Orthodox Church also progressively increased throughout his reign. He allowed more devout Orthodox practices to continue against the wishes of the Church, and though he technically remained a member of the Church himself, Peter simply viewed it as a state institution. With that in mind, Peter implemented church reforms that lasted until the Bolshevik Revolution of 1918, including a preference for Western-educated theologians and the replacement of the patriarch with an exarch who held the seat but had no real power.

Peter's reign rapidly transformed Russia, but the massive debts and the changing culture caused plenty of unrest among his empire. Faced with high taxes, warfare, forced labor and changes in their religious beliefs and practices, many peasants and deserting soldiers simply fled into the less-controlled southern reaches of Russia. In these faraway areas along the Volga River, rebellions were common; in 1705, the citizens of Astrachan revolted, having heard that Peter would ban marriages among Russian men for seven years. Peter offered them leniency, but the rebellion continued and the amnesty was withdrawn. Further rebellions followed in 1708, but all of them were rapidly and violently suppressed by the Russian army.

Shortly after the 1703 victory at the fortress of Nienchanz, Peter began work on a fortress to protect the mouth of the Neva River, but construction was not an easy process. The land was swamp-like, working conditions were poor, and the marsh flooded frequently, forcing imported workers to live in hastily constructed shantytowns that were racked by disease. This fortress, called the Fortress of Peter and Paul, was a replacement for the badly damaged fortress at Nienchanz, originally built in timber and earth but rebuilt in stone between 1706 and 1740.

Soon after construction on the fortress began, a simple three-room cabin was built on site for Peter himself. The cabin, built without fireplaces or heating stoves, contained a living room, study and bedroom, providing enough of a home for Peter, Catherine and their children during the early phase of the construction of St. Petersburg. The wooden cabin was intended to look like a stone home in the Dutch style, but stone was not available in the area. The wood of the cabin was painted to give it a finished and European appearance, and today a red brick pavilion encloses and protects the original structure.

In November 1704, Peter moved the main naval shipyards from Lake Ladoga to St. Petersburg in order to avoid the long and often damaging voyage from the inland lake to the coastline. Several large sheds on the site held living quarters and workshops, while open areas provided ample space for shipbuilding and nearby wharves provided space to outfit the completed hulls. Stone ramparts and moats were built soon after to protect the shipyards and offices.

It was probably around this same time that Peter began to envision this new settlement as more than just a shipyard and military installation, but further building made clear that he envisioned something larger by 1710. That year, a simple wooden church, the Church of the Holy Trinity, was built to meet the religious needs of the small, but growing community. Trinity Square, a space between Peter's cabin and the fortress, was subsequently designed to be the center of the city and named after the Church of the Holy Trinity. Inns, taverns, and homes for the nobility were also located in Trinity Square, as was the government printing office and the city's first hospital. In 1712, while he was still residing in St. Petersburg, Peter ordered the newly formed Russian senate to come to the city, bringing in nobles and wealth.

A painting by Alexandre Benois entitled *Peter the Great Meditating the Idea of Building St Petersburg at the Shore of the Baltic Sea.*

Work began on the Peter and Paul cathedral in 1713 to meet the spiritual needs of this now much larger community, and a single large market owned by the Tsar himself served the city, which continued to expand as Peter forced members of the nobility to move to St. Petersburg. Workers forced to the city to work on government building projects often stayed after their six months ended, taking jobs building homes and businesses for the newly imported residents, and by 1714 official accounts indicate that there were more than 34,000 buildings in the city.

Building in St. Petersburg was costly, as all supplies, including stone and timber, had to be imported from elsewhere in Russia. Further costs were incurred by Peter's taste for Western architecture; the nobility were required to build in the English style along the left bank of the Neva River, using beams and plaster, and wealthier nobles were expected to build two-story homes. Peter's own builder provided architectural plans for both single and two-story homes in the Western style to help the nobility build according to Peter's plan and regulations.

While the city soon took on a cosmopolitan, European appearance, significant problems remained. There was little arable land for grain and livestock, so merchants had to import food at high costs, and local woodlands provided only limited access to game, mushrooms and berries. If the wagons and sleds carrying food from other regions of Russia were late in arriving, prices increased and famine became a risk. Making matters worse, wild animals, including bears and wolves, occasionally attacked the settlers.

The city was separated into various sections and islands by the Neva River, which posed its own set of problems because the river was often rough and stormy. Private boats and 20 public ferries were available to allow for river crossings, and for a number of years Peter required the ferries to try to sail the river without using oars, relenting only after several drowning. On the other hand, one advantage to this city design was that the river froze in winter, making travel significantly easier for people and carts.

In 1716, the French architect and engineer Jean-Baptiste Alexandre LeBlond arrived in St. Petersburg to serve as the new Architect General of Russia. He had an expansive and involved plan for the city, including a system of canals to make transit throughout the city safer and easier, but while his plan was good, the construction attempt resulted in overly narrow and inefficient canals that could not be used (though it did provide St. Petersburg with the nickname "the Venice of the North"). But Peter did not recognize or acknowledge the problems affecting the city, as he loved the location, the water surrounding it, the access to the port, and the modern, European style of the new construction.

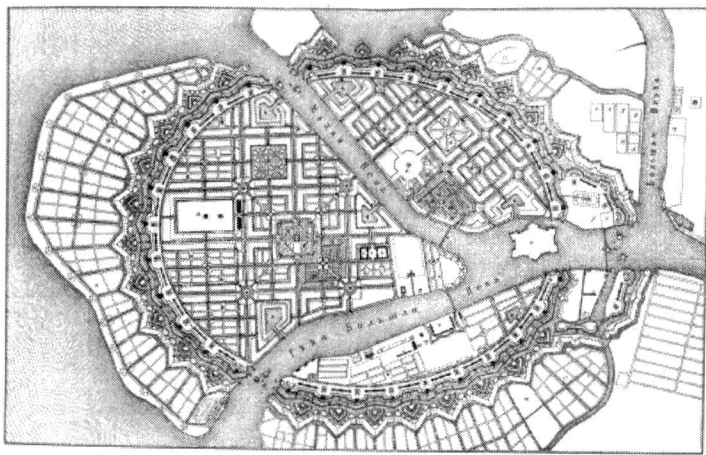

LeBlond's design for St. Petersburg

Alexander Menshikov built the Menshikov Palace on Vasilevsky Island, which had been given to him by Peter. The Menshikov Palace was the finest residence in St. Petersburg and was used for official functions of all sorts, as Peter's own residences were not large enough to accommodate royal banquets, receptions and gatherings. While much of the early 18th century architecture of St. Petersburg has been lost, the Menshikov Palace remains a stunning example of

Peter's city and its European-style architecture.

Given the difficulties with the islands in the Neva, the majority of government buildings and residences were on the mainland along the bank of the Neva, while Peter's own winter palace, a two-story wooden building, sat alongside the other homes of the nobility on the left bank. It would eventually be torn down in 1721 to be replaced by a stone structure. Peter and Catherine's summer palace, located somewhat further from the city, was a 14 room home, with Peter's rooms on the lower floor and Catherine's on the upper. Her rooms were regal, but his were modest and unimposing. The summer palace has been restored, and today it remains much the same way it was in Peter's time. LeBlond designed a formal, French-style summer garden at the palace, including a small menagerie, fountains and a variety of plants. Badly damaged in 1777, the modern garden reflected a late eighteenth century style and sensibility, inspired by more relaxed English gardens rather than the formal style Peter favored. Perhaps not surprisingly, LeBlond's design for St. Petersburg would be called "a plan conceived by a gardener".

LeBlond died when he was just 39, but he left behind the drawings and plans for the palace of Peterhof on the coast of the Baltic Sea. Peter first built a small, two room cottage at the site, using it as a space to spend the night in bad weather, before replacing it with a small wooden house called Strelna. These modest beginnings belied the fact that Peterhof was intended to become a palace that would rival Versailles and Menshikov's nearby country estate, Oranienbaum. It was also to be a testament to Peter's lifelong love of the sea. Fountains and canals integrate water into the gardens, while large French windows allow one to step out onto terraces overlooking the water from any room. Even the interior decor favored ships and the sea. It soon became Peter's favorite retreat.

Not long before his death, Peter funded the construction of a number of public cultural institutions in the city of St. Petersburg. The city became home to a library, art gallery and zoo, and a science museum provided access to a large collection of animal specimens. Wine and coffee were provided and admission was free, as Peter hoped the people would visit and learn from his collections. Peter also founded the Academy of Science in St. Petersburg, though he would not live to see it grow and thrive.

By 1715, Peter's hard drinking and insistence on a fairly hardscrabble lifestyle on battlefields and city outposts had all taken a toll on his health. When Peter returned to Western Europe in 1716 and 1717 to attend the wedding of his niece Catherine to the Duke of Mecklenberg in Germany, he made several state visits and hoped traveling in the warmer climate would improve his health. While his epilepsy was of relatively little concern to his physicians, he now had frequent fevers that lasted for several weeks, and court physicians suggested that the mineral waters near Hanover, Germany would improve his constitution and health.

Catherine, once again in the early stages of pregnancy, left behind their daughters Anne and Elizabeth, as well as an infant son, to accompany him. Faced with winter and another pregnancy and delivery for his wife, Peter opted to proceed to Amsterdam for the coldest months. Catherine followed in her own carriage and with her own guard, but stopped to deliver her child and recover along the Dutch border. Sadly, the infant did not survive and Catherine's recovery was difficult, forcing her to take plenty of time to convalesce. When she did recover from the birth, Catherine found Peter in bed with a fever, as he had been for several months. He would not recover until the end of the winter that year.

In 1717, Peter planned to visit France, where the "Sun King", Louis XIV, had recently died and France was under the rule of a regent, Philippe, duc d'Orleans, during the childhood of Louis XV. Philippe favored a pro-English diplomatic policy, and though France had been a traditional ally of Sweden, Peter hoped that he could secure an alliance with France. Peter traveled to Paris with a small delegation, and while the French questioned his manners, they were charmed when Peter picked up the boy king, hugged and kissed him. His friendly and kind treatment of the boy impressed the French court, even if they found him personally abrupt and prone to mood swings, but Peter's attempt at creating a French alliance failed. This was likely due to no fault of his own; relations between Russia and England were not good at the time, and France chose an English alliance over a Russian one.

Chapter 8: The Succession

Peter's oldest son and heir, Alexei, was born shortly after his ill-fated marriage to Eudoxia in 1690, and his relationship with his father was strained from the very beginning, probably through no fault of his own. Alexei's education was frequently neglected in favor of war, and Peter showed little interest in the boy, likely as a result of the fact he had no use for Eudoxia. Nevertheless, contemporaries indicated that Alexei was both bright and capable. He was also the opposite of Peter; Alexei was a quiet and religious boy who preferred Moscow to St. Petersburg and showed little interest in warfare, the military or fortifications.

Alexei

Alexei developed a close circle of associates in Moscow, including relatives of his Aunt Sophia, during his late teens, and in 1706 he was taken to visit his mother by one of those relatives. He had not seen Eudoxia since he was eight years old, which had only weakened his already poor relationship with his father. When he was 19, Peter sent Alexei to Dresden to get a Western education and to remove him from his friends in Moscow. While Alexei was obedient, he remained a devout Orthodox Christian, even begging his confessor in Russia to send an Orthodox priest in disguise since his father would not allow him one.

As fate would have it, Peter's successor would be a byproduct of the fact that the Tsar forced a Western bride upon his son. Alexei was married to Princess Charlotte of Wolfenbuttel of Germany in 1712, and like Peter and Eudoxia, the newly married couple had no use for each other. After being treated badly by Alexei, Charlotte died giving birth to the future Peter II of Russia in 1714.

Alexei had begun to drink heavily as a teen, and by the time he was settled in St. Petersburg he frequently had to be carried home drunk. His hatred of Peter reached a point that he even occasionally feigned illness and attempted to injure himself to avoid Peter. Alexei had no desire to rule or accept his duties as Tsarevich, and this was more than Peter could bear. When Alexei offered to renounce the throne, Peter countered by offering him the choice between keeping his position in the succession or entering a monastery. After spending several months considering his choice, Alexei fled to the Austrian Empire along with his mistress, where they were hidden in a remote castle by the Austrian Emperor.

Peter searched for Alexei, but this was more out of his concern and anger than any notion of love, because Peter believed the defection put his reign at stake. When he located Alexei, he moved him to Naples, and it was there in September 1717 that Russian diplomats met with Alexei and persuaded him to return to St. Petersburg, at which time he was formally pardoned and denounced. Alexei was also required to provide his father with details relating to conspiracies against the Tsar, and a large number of arrests followed, along with torture and many brutal deaths.

In June 1718, the Tsarevich was arrested, tried, and tortured himself, thanks to testimony provided by his mistress. Though there was no evidence or facts aside from hearsay, she alleged that Alexei told her, "I shall bring back the old people and choose myself new ones according to my will; when I become sovereign I shall live in Moscow and leave Saint Petersburg simply as any other town; I won't launch any ships; I shall maintain troops only for defense, and won't make war on anyone; I shall be content with the old domains. In winter I shall live in Moscow, and in summer in Iaroslav." Alexei's alleged statement seemed almost too perfectly crafted to oppose everything Peter loved and advocated, but he was nevertheless sentenced to death. Before he was put to death, however, he died on June 26, a few days after the already ill Tsarevich had been whipped 40 times.

A painting depicting Peter interrogating his son Alexei

By 1722, Peter had begun to look for husbands for his two surviving daughters, Anne and Elizabeth, who were both considered remarkably pretty, well-educated and desirable even after they had battled smallpox. Still, his plan suggested that he did not intend them to inherit his throne. The presumed heir was Tsarevich Alexei's son with his wife Charlotte, the future Peter II, but Peter did not want his grandson to inherit and had another possibility in mind: his wife. In 1722, Peter decreed that the sovereign held the right to delegate his successor, regardless of inheritance or birth, and Catherine was formally crowned in 1724. However, a scandal in her household reduced her power and control, which caused a rare disagreement between the close couple.

The two eventually reconciled, but by then, the 52 year old Tsar was in failing health. His epilepsy had worsened, he suffered from weakness in his left arm, and from 1722 onward he suffered from a variety of urinary complications, including a large kidney stone in 1724. It is likely that these urinary difficulties were the cause of his long-lasting and frequent fevers over the years.

Peter died of inflammation of the bladder and intestine on January 28, 1725, having taken the last rites of the Orthodox Church, pardoned state prisoners and reconciled with both his wife and old friend Menshikov. True to form, Catherine succeeded her husband and was proclaimed the sole ruler of the state the following day. During her reign, she continued her husband's policies with Menshikov's support and assistance. If it was unclear just how much Peter had transformed the customs of Russia, the proof can be found in the fact that Catherine, born a peasant, became the first woman to rule the Russian state in her own right.

"The Bronze Horseman", the famous equestrian statue of Peter in St. Petersburg

Bibliography

An Illustrated History of St. Petersburg. *Saint-Petersburg.com.* http://www.saint-petersburg.com/history/index.asp (accessed on October 3, 2012).

Anderson, M.S. Peter the Great. Thames & Hudson, London, 1978.

Bell, J. Travels from St. Petersburg into Russia to Diverse Parts of Asia. 2 vols. Glasgow, 1763.

Bogoslovsky, M.M. Peter the First: Materials for a Biography. 5 vols. Leningrad, 1940-8

Graham, Stephen. Peter the Great: A Life of Peter I of Russia. Ernest Benn, London, 1929.

Grey, Ian. Peter the Great: Emperor of All Russia. J.B. Lippincott, Philadelphia & New York, 1960.

Hughes, Lindsay. *Peter the Great: A Biography*. New Haven, CT: Yale University, 2004.

Kliuchevsky, Vasili. Peter the Great. St. Martin's, New York, 1958.

Massie, Robert K. *Peter the Great: His Life and World*. New York, NY: Modern Library, 2012.

Catherine the Great

Chapter 1: Catherine's Childhood

Young Catherine soon after her arrival in Russia, by Louis Caravaque

"I will live to make myself not feared." – Catherine the Great

The woman who would become Russia's most famous queen was not even Russian. Catherine the Great was born Sophia Augusta Fredericka on May 2, 1729 to Prince Christian August of Anhalt-Zerbst, an officer in the German army, and Johanna Elizabeth of Holstein-Gottorp, daughter of the wealthy Duke and Duchess of Brunswick. Still a bride of 17 when her first child was born, Johanna was not entirely happy with her much older husband, and the sour relations between the two were only exacerbated by the difficult birth of Sophia. It took nearly 5 months for Johanna to recover from a childbirth that nearly killed her, and that simply piled onto a life that she found relatively bored compared to her earlier years growing up at court in Brunswick. While the child's parents had their marital strife, little Sophia would spend most of her first year of life being cared for exclusively by her wet nurse.

Christian August

Unfortunately, Sophia's life did not improve any when her brother, Wilhelm Christian, was born a year and a half later. Unhealthy at birth and crippled for life, he soon became their mother's favorite, and even after he died at the young age of 12, the devastated Johanna continued to show little interest in Sophia or her two remaining siblings,

While Sophia's mother had little interest in her children, their governess, Elizabeth Cardel, took her duties as primary caregiver much more seriously. Called Babet, Cardel inspired a lifelong love for the French language in her young pupil, though any romantic notions the young girl formed from French literature were carefully balance by the long passages of Scripture her German tutor, a local pastor, had her memorize.

By the time she was 8 years old, Sophia's bright and curious personality had attracted her mother's attention, and Johanna began bringing the child with her as she traveled to visit wealthier relatives. Both mother and daughter already considered Sophia a potential marriageable asset, which in this era provided the prospect of improving both of their lives. Though she was not considered a pretty child at 13, Sophia was showing the promise of growing into an attractive woman, and her quick intellect, leadership skills, and warmth made her an appealing potential match.

Johanna

Johanna's own status improved during the early 1740s when Christian August received a promotion to field marshal in the Prussian army and succeeded as ruler of Anhalt-Zerbst. The family now lived in a small baroque palace and was more financially secure than they had been in the past. With that, the options for a suitable husband for her daughter increased.

Chapter 2: Catherine the Bride

"A great wind is blowing, and that gives you either imagination or a headache." – Catherine the Great

One of Sophia's best prospects for a royal marriage lay in Russia, as Johanna's family had numerous ties to the Russian throne, currently held by the Empress Elizabeth, who had seized power in 1741. Elizabeth's older sister had been married to Johanna's cousin, and she herself had been betrothed to Johanna's older brother. Johanna wrote to Elizabeth expressing her congratulations in 1741 and the two began to correspond regularly. Elizabeth sent Johanna a richly jeweled miniature portrait as a sign of her favor and Johanna sent a portrait of Sophia in return and later asked Elizabeth to stand as godmother for her youngest child. Catherine the Great would eventually become known for her political intrigue and cunning, but it was her mother who was angling for her to become empress of Russia at this time.

Following her rise to power, Elizabeth named Peter Ulrich of Holstein, the son of her dead sister, Grand Duke of Russia. Then the Crown Prince of Sweden, Peter was pale, sickly and both emotionally and physically undeveloped for his age. He had poor manners, was uninterested in learning and loved to eat. He enjoyed military drills and playing with his toy soldiers, but he was not well enough for actual military training. He could speak French, Swedish and German, but he had no real aptitude for any other subjects. Peter enjoyed playing the violin, but had not been properly taught and therefore played poorly. After his father's death, an army official, Otto Brummer, took charge of his care, and Brummer was cruel to the boy, punishing him harshly and frequently refusing him food. Peter responded to this ill treatment by becoming both fearful and cruel himself, torturing animals and treating servants unkindly.

Peter

After naming him her heir, Elizabeth brought Peter to St. Petersburg at once, accompanied by Brummer, and she forced him to renounce his claim to the Swedish throne in favor of Russia's crown. She also assigned him new tutors and dancing and music instructors, but the harm to the young boy had already been done. Peter had no interest in anything Russian and actively objected to the notion of becoming Tsar of Russia. Instead, he remained firmly under Brummer's thumb.

In the meanwhile, Elizabeth named Johanna's brother heir to the Swedish throne and also contacted her friend about arranging a marriage between the future czar and Sophia, hoping that a German bride would help him to mature and focus on his duties in Russia. In January 1744, Johanna received a letter from the imperial court requesting she and Sophia present themselves as soon as possible, and the letter also included travel instructions and a letter of credit to cover the cost of the journey. Soon after, a letter arrived from Frederick II of Prussia clarifying that he hoped for a marriage between Sophia and Peter, and naturally Johanna was thrilled at her daughter's prospects.

Empress Elizabeth

Sophia's father, Christian August, was not invited to join the family, presumably because everyone believed that he would object to the match for religious reasons. While Russian royalty had, for centuries, refused to marry outside the Russian Orthodox Church, this policy had changed under Peter the Great. Thus, Sophia's Protestant upbringing would not be any hindrance to her marriage to Peter, and the absence of Christian August indicates Elizabeth and Frederick II clearly felt that Johanna could make this decision independently and would overcome any of her husband's objections. Christian August, who had always been fond of his daughter, gave his reluctant approval but left the details of planning the trip to his wife. As Johanna prepared to leave, she spent most of her travel budget on new dresses and items for herself, providing Sophia with a trousseau smaller than that of a girl from the local village. Even worse Johanna refused to allow Sophia to tell her beloved governess of their plan. Instead, in less than ten days, the family said their goodbyes and Sophia left for Berlin and an audience with Frederick II of Prussia.

Sophia said goodbye to her father 50 miles from Berlin. Both cried at their parting, and Sophia's letters home to her father show her love and respect for the quiet and modest man. Johanna and Sophia traveled on without him, taking only a few attendants and traveling under assumed names. The journey was a difficult one because the wet winter prevented them from using the quick-moving sleighs, but Sophia considered the journey a great adventure and was excited about the potential for her new life in Russia.

For his part, Frederick II, needed an alliance with Russia to shore up his nearly continuous war with Austria and saw the young German princess as a key means of creating that alliance. When they reached Berlin, Johanna presented herself but would not introduce Sophia. The king finally ordered the girl be provided with one of his sister's gowns and brought before him. Sophia sat alone at the king's table, where he found her both intelligent and charming. This was the only time the two great monarchs would meet.

Frederick the Great

A month after they left their home in Anhalt-Zerbst, the small party reached the Russian city of Riga and began to travel under their own names. The snow was heavier here, and they replaced their heavy carriages with elegant imperial sleighs, arriving in St. Petersburg on February 3, 1744. While the Empress Elizabeth was not present, mother and daughter were warmly welcomed by the court and outfitted with new Russian wardrobes in preparation for their eventual meeting with the Empress.

They set out a few days later for Moscow, hoping to reach the the Kremlin in time for Grand Duke Peter's 16th birthday celebration. The imperial sleighs moved quickly and the roads were good, allowing them to make the journey in only four days and arrive to a warm welcome in Moscow. Elizabeth had high hopes for the young princess, and, as she was a bit of a romantic who had chosen her lovers herself, hoped for a happy marriage for the two young people. Peter soon became friends with Sophia, but that was the extent of their relationship; Sophia soon realized that Peter was very much a child, more interested in games and toys than marriage or rule. Nevertheless, she was a remarkably practical young woman and played the only role she could in Peter's life, but her own memoirs present him as an unwise young man more than willing to display his love of Prussia rather than his loyalty to Russia.

Sophia chronicled Peter in a variety of negative ways in her memoirs:

"The Grand Duke appeared to rejoice at the arrival of my mother and myself. I was in my fifteenth year. During the first ten days he paid me much attention. Even then and in that short time, I saw and understood that he did not care much for the nation that he was destined to rule, and that he clung to Lutheranism, did not like his entourage, and was very childish. I remained silent and listened, and this gained me his trust. I remember him telling me that among other things, what pleased him most about me was that I was his second cousin, and that because I was related to him, he could speak to me with an open heart. Then he told me that he was in love with one of the Empress's maids of honor, who had been dismissed from court because of the misfortune of her mother, one Madame Lopukhina, who had been exiled to Siberia, that he would have liked to marry her, but that he was resigned to marry me because his aunt desired it. I listened with a blush to these family confidences, thanking him for his ready trust, but deep in my heart I was astonished by his imprudence and lack of judgment in many matters…

They raised the Prince for the throne of Sweden in a court that was too large for the country in which it was located and that was divided into several factions, which hated each other and vied to control the Prince's mind, which each faction wanted to shape. As a result, these factions inspired in him the reciprocal hatred they felt against the individuals they opposed…

From the age of ten, Peter III was partial to drink…

The education of Peter III was undermined by a clash of unfortunate circumstances. I will relate what I have seen and heard, and that in itself will clarify many things. I saw Peter III for the first time when he was eleven years old, in Eutin at the home of his guardian, the Prince Bishop of Lübeck. Some months after the death of Duke Karl Friedrich, Peter III's father, the Prince Bishop had in 1739 assembled all of his family at his home in Eutin to have his ward brought there. My grandmother, mother of the Prince Bishop, and my mother, sister of this same Prince, had come there from Hamburg with me. I was ten years old at the time.... It was then that I heard it said among this assembled family that the young duke was inclined to drink, that his attendants found it difficult to prevent him from getting drunk at meals, that he was restive and hotheaded, did not like his attendants and especially Brümmer, and that otherwise he showed vivacity, but had a delicate and sickly appearance. In truth, his face was pale in color and he seemed to be thin and of a delicate constitution. His attendants wanted to give this child the appearance of a mature man, and to this end they hampered and restrained him, which could only inculcate falseness in his conduct as well as his character..."

Sophia soon understood that she needed to please Empress Elizabeth more than Peter, and she set about immersing herself in the culture of her current country. She embraced her studies of Russia, both in terms of language and religion, and devoted herself to her study, even rising at night to practice the language. Her devotion to the language and faith impressed the court, and when she became ill the Empress herself nursed her back to health while Johanna ignored her daughter's needs.

On June 28, 1744, some months after she had recovered, Sophia officially converted to the Orthodox faith. At the ceremony, Sophia appeared pale and fatigued after three days of fasting, but she wore a scarlet gown made in the style of the Empress Elizabeth's and spoke well, reciting her vows in Russian. Her quick mind helped her to memorize the speech as she had so many others during her childhood. That day, Sophia became Ekaterina or Catherine, her new name chosen for her by Elizabeth. The betrothal ceremony, including costly rings presented by the Empress, took place the following day at the Kremlin.

Catherine soon had an income and a small court of her own but continued to function primarily as a playmate for her fiancé. When some courtier approached her and asked her to help correct his behavior, she refused, realizing that she needed to maintain his favor in the court for her own success. Meanwhile, Johanna was present in the court and at the betrothal but was displeased by the ceremony and her daughter's new rank as her superior in the court. As it turned out, Johanna had already been disgraced by her participation in court intrigues, and though Elizabeth continued to treat her well and send her gifts, Johanna was no longer welcomed at court. Her relationship with both her daughter and Peter also deteriorated during this time. In particular, Johanna disliked Peter and often took her rage out on her daughter, which actually had the perverse effect of bringing Peter and Catherine closer together once they began commiserating over the mistreatment they had both experienced. Unfortunately for them, Johanna would have to remain until after the wedding.

Peter's doctors, stating that the boy was not yet sexually mature, delayed the marriage by a full year, but Elizabeth still wanted to show off the future couple. In order to show her new family to the people, Elizabeth planned a pilgrimage across Russia, travelling by foot while the young couple held court in a carriage of their own. Johanna was horrified by the lack of court protocol, as was Peter's unwelcome supervisor, Brummer.

Portrait by George Christoph Grooth of the Grand Duchess Catherine circa 1745

While Elizabeth was fond of young Catherine, she was also a jealous woman. As Catherine's social status grew, Elizabeth became angry and lashed out at the girl over her debts. This was somewhat hypocritical since Elizabeth herself typically spent more lavishly than Catherine did.

In the fall of 1744, Peter contracted measles, and as soon as he recovered Elizabeth ordered the court moved from Moscow to St. Petersburg. Unfortunately, Peter was still weak and became ill once again, forcing Elizabeth to come to Peter and nurse the boy through smallpox for a six week period. Peter would not be well enough to reach St. Petersburg until late February of 1745.

Even as Elizabeth sat by Peter's sickbed, Johanna continued to cause problems in court. She objected to the fact that she and Catherine had separate rooms and believed Catherine's apartments were nicer than her own, which antagonized courtiers and also ensured Catherine and Johanna grew progressively further apart. Rumors began to circulate of an affair between Johanna and one of the counts in the court, and the events later that winter suggested the possibility when Johanna became pregnant and miscarried.

While Peter was sick and Johanna carried on, Johanna and Catherine were kept away from the boy out of fear of contagion, but when she finally saw her fiancé again, Catherine found his pock-marked face and body hideous. However, she had no intention of breaking her engagement; she was marrying the throne, not the boy who would inherit it. Even so, her reaction to his appearance destroyed their tenuous young friendship, and having been away from Catherine, Peter became even more child-like. Through much of 1745, Peter remained in his rooms, forcing his servants to engage in senseless military drills and playing with his toy soldiers. In May, Peter moved to the Summer Palace with Empress Elizabeth, leaving Catherine privately saddened by the lack of attention.

Against the wishes of Peter's physicians, Elizabeth set their wedding date for July 1745, despite the fact Peter's health continued to be frail and she needed a healthy, strong heir for the Russian throne. The wedding preparation began at once, with deliveries of cloth and other supplies as well as sketches and retellings of French weddings at Versailles. When the wedding finally took place on August 21, 1745, both bride and groom wore elaborate garments of cloth of silver. Catherine's memoirs described it as an exhausting and painful day, though she also noted that she still had her eye on the prize: "As this day approached, I grew more deeply melancholic. My heart did not foresee great happiness; ambition alone sustained me. At the bottom of my soul I had something, I know not what, that never for a single moment let me doubt that sooner or later I would succeed in becoming the sovereign Empress of Russia in my own right…"

Chapter 3: Catherine the Mother

"One cannot always know what children are thinking. Children are hard to understand, especially when careful training has accustomed them to obedience, and experience has made them cautious in their conversation with their teachers. Will you not draw from this the fine maxim that one should not scold children too much, but should make them trustful, so that they will not conceal their stupidities from us?" – Catherine the Great

Neither Catherine nor Peter was given any helpful or substantial instruction regarding marriage or marital intimacy. Peter had some vague, coarse conversations with his servants, while Catherine was unaware of even the most basic physical mechanics of sexuality. When Catherine asked her mother for information, she was harshly reprimanded, and when Peter finally came to bed on their wedding night, he fell asleep. The marriage would remain unconsummated for nine years.

There were most likely both psychological and physiological reasons for the couple's failure to consummate their marriage. Only two weeks after the wedding, Peter announced that he had fallen in love with one of Elizabeth's ladies-in-waiting. However, as the months passed and Catherine did not become pregnant, the blame fell on her shoulders. A woman, Madame Choglokova, was assigned to supervise the marriage bed and improve the marital relationship, but she made no attempt to do so. Catherine noted of Choglokova:

"At the end of May the Empress placed with me as chief governess Madame Choglokova, one of her maids of honor. This was a serious blow for me. I cried a great deal when she arrived and for the rest of the day; I had to be bled the following day. The morning before my bloodletting, the Empress came into my room, and seeing my red eyes, said to me that young women who did not love their husbands always cried, but that my mother had assured her that I had no aversion to marrying the Grand Duke, and that besides, she would not have forced me to do it, but that since I was married, I should not cry anymore.

The following day the Grand,Duke took me aside after dinner, and I saw clearly that he had been informed that Madame Cboglokova had been placed with me because I did not love him. But as I told him, I did not understand how they believed they would increase my tenderness for him by giving me this woman. Madame Choglokova was believed to be extremely virtuous because at that time she loved her husband adoringly; she had married him out of love. Such a fine example, placed before me, was perh aps meant to persuade me to do the same. We will see whether this succeeded.

Madame Choglokova was a gambler. She urged me to play faro like all the others. All of the Empress's favorites usually participated when they were not in Her Imperial Majesty's apartment. Besides this, also on behalf of Her Imperial Majesty, she gave me three thousand rubles to play faro. The ladies had noticed that I was short of money and had told the Empress. I asked her to thank Her Imperial Majesty for her Generosity."

Catherine reconciled with her mother after the wedding, but Johanna no longer served a role in the court and soon returned to Germany. The Empress sent gifts for her departure and gave Johanna a generous amount of money to pay her debts, and in return Johanna carried a letter to Frederick ordering him to recall his ambassador, indicating a clear break between Prussia and Russia. She left in disgrace and would, after the death of her husband, lose the small principality of Zerbst in Germany. Johanna died in exile in Paris.

Over the next few years, Elizabeth isolated the couple in the hopes it would force them to find solace in one another. While they did spend more time together, the nature of their relationship did not change, perhaps because they were closely supervised day and night. While Peter shared Catherine's bed, he played with his beloved toy soldiers, smuggled in by an ally in their small court. The situation within the court and their marriage did not improve and Peter grew progressively more difficult both personally and within their relationship, even maintaining a kennel of dogs in their room and routinely abusing the animals against Catherine's wishes and attempted interventions. Catherine wrote about one particularly strange anecdote that documented how difficult Peter could be:

"Toward the end of carnival, the Empress returned to the city. The first week of Lent, we began to make our devotions. Wednesday evening I was supposed to go bathe in Madame Choglokova's house, but the evening before, she came into my room, where the Grand Duke was too, and conveyed to him as well on the Empress's behalf the order to go bathe. Now, not only did he have a great dislike for bathing and all the other Russian customs or national habits, he even mortally detested them. He said quite firmly that he would do no such thing. She was also very stubborn and blunt in her speech, and told him that this would be disobeying Her Imperial Majesty. He declared that he could not be ordered to do what was repugnant to his nature, that he knew that the baths, to which he had never been, did not agree with him, that he did not want to die and that he held life most dear, and that the Empress would never force him to go. Madame Choglokova shot back that the Empress would know how to punish his disobedience. At this he became incensed. Finally she departed, saying that she was going to report this conversation word for word to the Empress. I do not know what she did, but she returned and the subject of argument changed, because she came to say that the Empress said that we did not have any children, that she was very angry, that she wanted to know which of us was at fault, and that she would send me a midwife and him a doctor. To all this she added many other outrageous remarks, of which we could make neither heads nor tails, and ended by saying that the Empress excused us from our devotions that week because the Grand Duke had said that the bath would undermine his health."

By 1750, Catherine and Peter returned to court in St. Petersburg, where Peter began a relationship with the Princess of Courland, a hunchbacked young woman. He also began to lash out at the Choglokovas and his aunt, and finally Elizabeth had had enough. The Empress announced she was sending a midwife and doctor to examine the couple, and now that the blame game was ready to start up, one of Catherine's ladies pointed out that since she was still a virgin, she could bear no fault, leading Madame Choglokova to in turn convince the Empress that the Grand Duchess was still a virgin. An experienced young woman was chosen to teach Peter about his duties in the marital bed, and though Peter was apparently successful with her, his interest in Catherine remained nonexistent.

Having endured several years of a loveless marriage, in 1752 Catherine became romantically involved with Sergei Saltykov, a handsome nobleman assigned to Peter's court. Peter became aware of the affair, but he was unconcerned by it and Madame Choglokova encouraged the relationship with Saltykov in the hopes Catherine might become pregnant. By December 1752, her plan had succeeded and Catherine was pregnant, but this pregnancy and a subsequent pregnancy both ended with miscarriages. Catherine documented her initial encounters with Saltykov in her memoirs:

"For some time already I had noticed that Chamberlain Sergei Saltykov was present more often than usual at court. He always came in the company of Lev Naryshkin. . . . Sergei Saltykov intimated to me the reason for his frequent appearances. At first I did not respond. When he spoke to me about it again, I asked him what he hoped to gain. He began to paint a picture as cheerful as it was passionate of the happiness he expected. I said, "And your wife, whom you married for love two years ago and with whom you are said to be madly in love, and she with you, what would she say?" He told me that all that glittered was not gold and that he was paying dearly for a moment of blindness. I did everything I could to make him change his mind. I truly believed that I was succeeding. I pitied him. But to my misfortune I listened to him. He was remarkably handsome and surely no one equaled him in the grand court, much less in ours.

Meanwhile, Madame Choglokova, who always had her favorite project in mind, which was to ensure the succession, took me aside one day and said, "Listen, I must speak to you very seriously." I kept my eyes and ears open as one might expect. She began with a long disquisition, as was her wont, about her devotion to her husband, about her virtue, about what must and must not be done to love each other and to promote or support conjugal bonds, and then she pushed on, saying that there were sometimes situations of major consequence that should be exceptions to the rule. I let her say everything she wanted without interrupting, not knowing where she was going with this, a bit astonished, and not knowing if she was setting a trap for me or if she spoke sincerely. As I was having these private reflections, she said, "You are going to see how much I love my country and how sincere I am. I do not doubt that you fancy someone. You are free to choose between S.S. and L.N. If I am not mistaken, it is the latter." At this I cried out, "No no, not at all." Then she said, "Well then, if it is not him, it is the other no doubt." I did not say a word, and she continued, "You will see that I will not make difficulties for you." I played dumb."

Saltykov

By 1754, Catherine became pregnant again, but by this time Choglokov had died and his wife had been relieved of her duties. They were replaced by the Shuvalovs, relatives of Elizabeth's latest lover. After a slow journey to the palace in St. Petersburg, Catherine delivered a healthy son in the Empress' own apartments, and Elizabeth took the baby and the midwife at once, leaving the young mother in her labor bed. Hours later, Countess Shuvalov arrived to find that Catherine had not even been allowed a drink of water or moved into her own bed. The midwife finally returned, but Catherine was not allowed to see her son for a week. When Saltykov was sent on a diplomatic mission, Catherine found herself completely alone, and she wound up recovering from the childbirth in near total isolation, spending the winter in the small room in which she had given birth rather than her own apartments. Catherine recounted the isolation in her memoirs:

"After the baptism of my son, there were parties, balls, illuminations, and fireworks at court, while I was still in bed, ill and suffering great boredom. To cap it all, the seventeenth day of my confinement was chosen to inform me of two very unpleasant pieces of news. The first was that Sergei Saltykov had been named to deliver the news of my son's birth to Sweden. The second was that Princess Gagarina's marriage had been set for the following week. That is, in plain language, I was immediately going to be separated from the two people I loved most in my entourage. I sank more than ever into my bed, where I did nothing but grieve."

Eventually Catherine returned to court, and her public life changed considerably in February 1755. The birth of her son provided her with security and status as the mother of the heir to the throne, even if she was rarely allowed to see him, and though she remained helpful to Peter, she no longer went out of her way to please him. For his own part, Saltykov had gone to Sweden and enjoyed himself as the widely acknowledged father of the heir to the Russian throne. While they continued to correspond, their relationship was over.

Chapter 4: Catherine the Lover

"To tempt, and to be tempted, are things very nearly allied, and, in spite of the finest maxims of morality impressed upon the mind, whenever feeling has anything to do in the matter, no sooner is it excited than we have already gone vastly farther than we are aware of, and I have yet to learn how it is possible to prevent its being excited. Flight alone is, perhaps, the only remedy; but there are cases and circumstances in which flight becomes impossible, for how is it possible to fly, shun, or turn one's back in the midst of a court? The very attempt would give rise to remarks. Now, if you do not fly, there is nothing, it seems to me, so difficult as to escape from that which is essentially agreeable. All that can be said in opposition to it will appear but a prudery quite out of harmony with the natural instincts of the human heart; besides, no one holds his heart in his hand, tightening or relaxing his grasp of it at pleasure." – Catherine the Great

In June 1755, Catherine met a Polish count, Stanislaus Poniatowski, as well as an English ambassador, Sir Charles Hanbury-Williams. Hanbury-Williams would become a dear friend and trusted advisor, while Poniatowski, his secretary, would share her bed. Hanbury-Williams provided a much-needed paternal influence for Catherine, as well as financial assistance for the indebted princess, while Poniatowski was cultured, well-read, devoted, and fundamentally innocent. Saltykov had been a known womanizer, but Poniatowski was the opposite and thus a naturally appealing target for the young woman.

Poniatowski

During the winter of 1755, Peter continued to play with his toy soldiers, drink heavily and socialize with women of poor reputation. When he took an unwelcome liking to one of Catherine's ladies, she managed him by reminding him that if they argued, Elizabeth would dismiss his favorites. Her control of the wayward prince grew as she handled more and more of the questions and concerns regarding the administration of his German principality, Holstein, and in the process she personally grew more assertive and sure of herself. She even began to publicly question his lies and claims regarding his own prowess.

By 1756, Empress Elizabeth was ill and frequently debilitated to the point that her doctors feared for her health. Catherine, along with her allies, began to make plans for the succession. While Peter could not be removed entirely, she could take a role as co-ruler and handle the management of the country. Peter was already widely deemed unfit to rule and Vice-Chancellor Bestuzhev drew up documents for this arrangement, but Catherine refused to respond or acknowledge them in writing, instead thanking him verbally. While her refusal to support his plan protected her in the event it became public, she also objected to the key role he planned for himself in the administration.

Elizabeth made it known in 1757 that she had concerns about Catherine's involvement with Holstein. While she held no illusions regarding Peter's abilities, she continued to hope that he would improve his behavior. Removed from one of her key roles in the Grand Duke's administration, Catherine opted to throw Peter a grand party, defining herself a new role in the court.

On September 8, 1757, Empress Elizabeth suffered a stroke, and though she recovered quickly, her ill health became public news and the court could no longer hide her condition. In October 1757, the new French ambassador succeeded in removing Hanbury-Williams from his ambassadorial office, but Poniatowski remained in the country on his own merits.

Catherine delivered her second living child, a daughter fathered by Poniatowski, in December 1757. While she was again ignored in favor of the child, she had arranged her own labor and recovery rooms, as well as post-partum care. A large screen shielded a comfortable seating area so her friends could visit during her recovery and join her for meals during her confinement. While Elizabeth took the child at once, Catherine was less bothered than she had been with the loss of her son. When her daughter Anna died 15 months later, only Elizabeth and Catherine attended the funeral.

Equestrian Portrait of Grand Duchess Catherine

Chapter 4: Catherine the Politician

Vice-Chancellor Bestuzhev, who had been both Catherine's enemy and ally during her years in Russia, fell from power early in 1758. With the support of the French ambassador (the Marquis l'Hopital), the head of the Secret Chancellory (Alexander Shuvalov), and Elizabeth's lover (Ivan Shuvalov), the Empress ordered Bestuzhev arrested. Several others in his close circle were arrested, and news of the arrests reached Catherine from Poniatowski. Bestuzhev's accusers had nothing specific with which to charge him, so they ultimately settled on a charge of lese-majeste or sowing discord between the Empress and the Grand Duke and Duchess. No evidence was found, and Bestuzhev was eventually allowed to retire to his own country estate.

Shuvalov

When Empress Elizabeth ordered Poniatowski recalled to Poland, he feigned illness and managed to remain in Russia, continuing to disguise himself and visit Catherine regularly. One night, as he returned from a nighttime visit, Peter's carriage met his and he was detained, but he was soon released with Shuvalov's assistance. However, his relationship with Catherine was now obvious to Peter, forcing Catherine to quickly intervene with Peter's mistress and cajole them into a warm and friendly conversation one night between the four of them. While Peter was pleased by this situation, Catherine realized that the very public nature of her relationship with Poniatowski placed her at additional risk and sent Poniatowski back to Poland herself, ending their romantic relationship.

Concerned with her personal loss and her own well-being, Catherine gathered all of her papers and burned them, asking her valet to witness the destruction. On the last day before Lent, Catherine announced she would attend the Russian theater, but Peter objected at once and refused her a carriage because he disliked the theater and wanted to enjoy the company of one of her ladies-in-waiting. In response to her situation, Catherine drafted a letter requesting permission to return home because her marriage had failed and asked Shuvalov to deliver it. Aware that the Empress could not send her home since she was a key political asset, this letter and what followed was a power play on Catherine's part, improving her access to resources within her own household and the court.

The following day, Catherine was informed that one of her few longtime attendants, Madame Vladislavova, had been dismissed. One of Catherine's ladies offered to try to intervene with her uncle and the Empress's confessor, Father Dubyansky, but Catherine feigned illness in order to meet with the confessor herself. While Catherine remained in bed, Father Dubyansky spoke with the Empress, encouraging her to meet with her one time protégé. Elizabeth granted her an audience on April 13, 1758.

Speaking in front of Ivan Shuvalov, Catherine again begged to be allowed to return home. Peter and Elizabeth were not receptive to her request, and Peter's behavior was so poor that Elizabeth called an end to the interview, privately telling Catherine that they would speak again. Alexander Shuvalov, who had heard the conversation while hiding behind a screen, visited Catherine's room some time later and assured her that she would have another audience with Elizabeth soon. When Catherine again met with Elizabeth more than a month later, the Empress treated her kindly and asked for details of Peter's life and behavior, but even though Catherine was restored to the Empress' favor, Peter still remained the heir.

As Elizabeth's health continued to decline, Catherine became a more prominent figure in the court, attracting the attention of Ivan Shuvalov. She also gained the support of Count Nikita Panin, her son Paul's tutor, and conspired with him to make Paul Elizabeth's heir rather than Peter. This would have made Catherine regent, allowing her to hold the throne herself through her son. Catherine also found an ally in Princess Catherine Dashkova, a popular court intellectual.

By far the most important of Catherine's new supporters was Lieutenant Gregory Orlov, a decorated soldier who soon became her secret lover. Orlov and Catherine were drawn together by physical passion, and in addition to the fact that their relationship was remarkably uncomplicated, with Orlov came the loyalty of his brothers and the guard they commanded. This immediately worked to Catherine's favor, as the Orlovs spread rumors about Peter among the ranks of the Russian Imperial Guard, saying that he was not only unfit to rule but loyal to his homeland of Germany and the empire of Prussia.

Orlov

In 1761, Catherine became pregnant with Orlov's child, and since Peter had been threatening to divorce her, she had no hopes that he would claim the child as his own. Thus she retired to her rooms and hid her pregnancy from the court. Meanwhile, Elizabeth was dying, and though she did not feel comfortable with Peter as her heir, she refused to change the order of succession. Catherine wrote, "It is impossible to say what Her Imperial Majesty Elizabeth Petrovna's last thoughts were about the succession, for she had no clear ideas on the subject. There is no doubt that she did not like P. III and considered him incapable of ruling; she knew he did not love the Russians, she thought of death with fear and horror, as well as of what would come after; but as she was slow in taking any decision, particularly in her last years, one can guess that she also hesitated on the question of the succession."

Prepared for the death of the Empress, Catherine even drafted a list of suggestions giving advice to Peter:

"1. It seems of the greatest importance that you should be informed, Sire, as exactly as possible, of the Empress's state of health, not relying upon hearsay, but with your ears wide open and with a complete grasp of the situation. If God disposes of her, you ought to be present at the event.

2. Having reached the scene and established that the event has taken place, you will emerge from her room, leaving behind you in the room a prominent national figure, who is capable of making all the arrangements suitable and customary on these occasions.

3. With the self-control of a general in command of an army, without embarrassment or confusion, you will send for:

4. The Chancellor and other members of the Council, and while waiting for them:

5. You will summon the captain of the guards and make him take the oath of loyalty to you on the cross and the Bible (if the formula of the oath is not decided upon you will use that of the Greek Church).

6. You will order the captain (in case the General-Adjutant is not in a position to appear or you have found it opportune to leave him, as mentioned above in 2, with the Empress's body) to go and

7. Announce to the Court guards the news of the death and your accession to the throne of your forefathers according to the rights you hold from God and Nature, at the same time ordering."

In December 1761, the Empress suffered a massive stroke but remained lucid, taking the last rites of the Orthodox Church before dying on Christmas Day. Upon her death, the Grand Duke became Peter III, Emperor of Russia, and Peter wasted no time in throwing grand banquets and parties to celebrate his new role as Emperor, behaving childishly at the various funeral rituals and consistently refusing to follow Orthodox Church traditions regarding mourning and grief. Though by law he became the official head of the Church, he disliked any institution that sought to control his behavior and soon laid claim to much of its property, in addition to issuing orders deeply at odds with Church tradition.

Although his personal behavior was poor, Peter's political behavior was sometimes moderate and appropriate. He gave amnesty to a number of Elizabeth's enemies and reduced taxes. Always the wannabe soldier, he took an immediate interest in the military, ordering them into Prussian style uniforms and making peace with Frederick II of Prussia at once before preparing to attack Denmark. In the process, he had managed to make two powerful enemies in less than two months: the Russian Orthodox Church and the Russian army.

In April 1762, Catherine delivered a son who was immediately taken out of the city to be raised in the home of her valet, Vasily Shkurin, and within 10 days she had begun to take an active role at court once again. However, she and Peter remained on very poor terms, and he treated his mistress, Elizabeth Vorontsova, as Empress. He soon began to insult Catherine in public and even attempted to have her arrested on one occasion. After this, Catherine realized how tenuous her position was and began, to actively plot against Peter.

By June, Catherine and her co-conspirators had a plan in place. However, on June 27, only days before they planned to arrest Peter, rumors began to spread of the conspiracy. Concerned that they would be found out, Catherine's allies rushed to Peterhof to bring her back to the capital and proclaim her Empress, even before arresting and removing Peter from power. Early in the morning of June 28, Alexis Orlov, one of Gregory's brothers, woke Catherine and informed her of the situation. She left at once, with her hair undone and wearing a simple black dress, traveling in a shabby hired carriage pulled by farm horses purchased along the way to replace the exhausted team. Thus the future empress of Russia entered her capital simply and made her way immediately to the solder's barracks, where the regiment chaplain administered oaths of loyalty to all present while the Archbishop of Novgorad proclaimed her the sovereign ruler in St. Petersburg later that same morning. Paul, now Catherine's heir, arrived at the Winter Palace and he was formally proclaimed heir to the throne. Thus Catherine was made, not the regent, but the Empress of all Russia.

As for Peter, he had traveled to the country estate of Peterhof that morning and reached the deserted palace in the afternoon. When rumors reached Peterhof late that afternoon, he sent men into St. Petersburg, but when they arrived and faced the cheering crowds, they swore allegiance to Catherine. Later that night, Peter, believing that the fortress of Kronstadt was secure, moved there with his mistress and her ladies, only to find that he was not welcome and that the men at the fortress had, like so many others, proclaimed Catherine their Empress. Peter continued on, finally reaching the summer palace at Oranieumbaum, where he dismissed many of those with him, having learned that Catherine marched toward him with an army. In a last ditch effort to preserve his power, he wrote a letter to Catherine apologizing for his behavior and offering to share his throne.

Meanwhile, Catherine proclaimed herself colonel of the Preobrazhensky Guard and, dressed in a borrowed Russian military uniform, led the march herself toward Peterhof. As they traveled, a young member of the horse guard, Gregory Potemkin, broke rank to give the Empress the sword knot from his uniform to replace the one missing from hers, securing his own place in history.

Catherine in the Preobrazhensky Regiment's uniform

After camping overnight, the army again set off early the following morning, and along the way Peter's chancellor reached Catherine with his letter. When she stated that there would be no reply, he himself abandoned his Emperor and immediately took an oath of allegiance to Catherine. When Peter heard of this final defection, he formally abdicated the throne, asking only to be allowed to go to Holstein with his mistress.

Upon arriving in Peterhof, Catherine was informed that Peter was already there with his mistress, Elizabeth Vorontsova. After saying goodbye to his longtime companion, Peter asked to see Catherine, who refused the request and instead sent orders to imprison him. Peter was taken under heavy guard to a small country estate of his choosing, Ropsha, and Alexis Orlov was placed in charge of the prisoner until a more permanent solution could be found. While there is no evidence that Catherine ever suggested Peter be killed, those around her were more than willing to dispose of him, and within a week he was dead, strangled after dinner by his guards. Orlov sent news of Peter's death to Catherine in a hastily written letter that she kept locked away for the remainder of her life. For her own part, Catherine opted to claim that Peter had died of natural causes, perhaps hemorrhoids or the result of excess drink.

Chapter 5: Catherine the Empress

Portrait of Empress Catherine circa 1770 by Ivan Sablukov

"As a ruler, Catherine professed a great contempt for system, which she said she had been taught to despise by her master Voltaire. She declared that in politics a capable ruler must be guided by "circumstances, conjectures and conjunctions." - The Encyclopædia Britannica

Though Catherine's coup was widely supported and she had no significant opposition among the military or nobility, she did not have a legal right to the throne. Since the time of Peter the Great, the emperor could appoint a successor, but she had not been lawfully appointed by her husband. On top of that, her son Paul, still in the care of his loyal tutor, was often ill, causing more worry about her grip on power and potential succession.

Catherine also dealt swiftly with other matters in her court, both great and small. In order to shore up her power, she treated past adversaries leniently and showered her supporters with gifts, paying special attention to the Orlov brothers. While Gregory Orlov hoped to marry her, Catherine had no interest in marriage. Princess Dashkova was angered by her own rank in the court even after being promoted, and she frequently complained that she was seated among inferiors. Catherine recalled Bestuzhev and provided him with quarters in the summer palace, while her old enemies, including Elizabeth Vostokova, were treated kindly.

Catherine also planned a grand coronation for herself in the Kremlin in Moscow, and the ceremony that took place on September 13, 1762 lasted for more than four hours. She spent the next nine months of her reign in Moscow, where she made essential changes to maintain the key support she required to rule successfully. She canceled the Russian alliance with Prussia, recalled troops from Denmark, and ordered Russian soldiers home. She also returned church property secularized by Peter and restored the traditions of the Russian Orthodox Church, at least for a time.

While Catherine was able to maintain the support she required, the Russian government faced several key challenges. The treasury was bankrupt and the costs of grain had doubled, placing many of its people at risk of starvation. To alleviate some of this suffering, Catherine gave the funds allocated to her own household to the state treasury and banned all exports of grain to reduce the cost of bread. Within just a few months, the cost of grain dropped substantially, helping to ensure adequate food supplies, and her popularity naturally rose among the people. She also ended the monopolies on trade goods begun by Peter the Great to lower the cost of these items and increase competition. And Catherine regularly interacted with the Russian Senate, though it was known by all involved that she retained absolute power as monarch.

With Peter dead, there remained only one other possible claimant to the throne other than her own son and heir, Paul. Ivan VI was the infant king deposed by Elizabeth at the beginning of her reign. Raised in prison, he was mentally unstable as a result of his upbringing, and he was also uneducated, making him quite unfit to rule. However, Catherine's enemies could still proclaim him the rightful emperor, and when Catherine visited Ivan, she found him unintelligible, but not utterly disabled. Thus, she ordered his imprisonment to continue, placing Panin in charge of overseeing him, and Panin ordered no medical care be given to the young man in the hopes he would conveniently die of natural causes. And just to be safe, his guards, as they had been under Empress Elizabeth, were ordered to kill him rather than allow a potential escape.

In the winter of 1764, Vasily Mirovich was assigned to the isolated fortress that had been home to Ivan VI for many years. Mirovich was a bitter young man and saw Ivan as a potential means of gaining both fame and fortune. When Mirovich attempted to free the prisoner, the guards, as ordered, killed Ivan and brought Mirovich to trial, where he was condemned to death for his actions.

Mirovich Standing over the Corpse of Ivan VI (1884). by Ivan Tvorozhnikov

Though head of the Russian Orthodox Church, Catherine soon began to rethink returning the property Peter had taken. The Church was immensely wealthy, and Catherine was uncomfortable with that much wealth being in the hand of any institution she did not control. Claiming to want the Church to have more social responsibility to the people of Russia, she created a Senate committee to tabulate its total wealth. The Senate suggested that the Church retain its wealth but pay a higher tax to the state, and though the Archbishop of Novgorod offered his support for this plan, others in the Church did not. Their opposition was met in a way that would set the tone for much of her reign; Catherine silenced and imprisoned anyone who was too vocal with their criticism.

In 1764, she officially brought the Church under state control once again, placing more than one million additional peasants under state rather than Church care. Because taxing church property dramatically increased the wealth of the state, she had the strong support of the nobility, a largely secular population. With the loss of property and revenue, many churches and monasteries were forced to close, and priests and church officials were forced to rely on and become salaried employees of the state. The Russian Orthodox Church would never regain its former status and standing.

As early as 1766, Catherine began to revise the Russian legal code. The law code in place was already more than a century old and many new, often contradictory, laws had been added, creating both chaos and confusion. Peter the Great had made significant reforms, but he had not placed many of these into writing. Catherine's *Nakaz* or *Instruction of her Imperial Majesty Catherine the Second for the Commission Charged with Comparing a Project of a New Code of Laws,* took more than two years to develop. In the *Nakaz*, Catherine defined Russia as an absolute but moderate monarchy, with its power limited by tradition, including the dominant religion of the land.

Catherine called a National Assembly, drawn from all the free people of Russia, to create a new law code for the country. Delegates were paid a salary, depending upon their social class, and both the nobility and free working classes all had a voice in the Assembly. Of course, they were only there to offer advice, since Catherine retained the right to make any laws she chose but frequently attended meetings, secluded behind a curtain.

The *Nakaz* laid out reasonable punishments for crime, reduced the use of the death penalty and condemned torture. While her advisers objected, Catherine acknowledged the humanity and basic rights of the serf, even if she could not change their standing or status because of the objections of the nobility. In the original draft of the *Nakaz*, Catherine included measures to allow serfs to buy their freedom, limited servitude to only six years and required that once freed, a serf remain free. While Catherine embraced many Enlightenment ideas, the *Nakaz* was reviewed by the National Assembly and later, a number of nobles. All measures intended to improve the standing of the Russian serfdom were removed.

Nevertheless, Catherine's *Nakaz* was the first time the people of Russia, on however limited a basis, had been able to participate in the Russian government. It also demonstrated the influence that Enlightenment thinking was having on her, and Catherine ultimately became well-acquainted with Voltaire, who she respected and admired greatly. Excerpts from the *Nakaz* spell out just how important it was to Catherine that Russian rulers wield power as enlightened and benevolent despots:

> "The Sovereign is absolute; for there is no other Authority but that which centers in his single Person, that can act with a Vigour proportionate to the Extent of such a vast Dominion.
>
> The Extent of the Dominion requires an absolute Power to be vested in that Person who rules over it. It is expedient so to be, that the quick Dispatch of Affairs, sent from distant Parts, might make ample Amends for the Delay occasioned by the great

Distance of the Places.

Every other Form of Government whatsoever would not only have been prejudicial to Russia, but would even have proved its entire Ruin.

It is better to be subject to the Laws under one Master, than to be subservient to many.

What is the true End of Monarchy? Not to deprive People of their natural Liberty; but to correct their Actions, in order to attain the supreme Good.

The Form of Government, therefore, which best attains this End, and at the same Time sets less Bounds than others to natural Liberty, is that which coincides with the Views and Purposes of rational Creatures, and answers the End, upon which we ought to fix a steadfast Eye in the Regulations of civil Polity.

The Intention and the End of Monarchy, is the Glory of the Citizens, of the State, and of the Sovereign.

But, from this Glory, a Sense of Liberty arises in a People governed by a Monarch; which may produce in these States as much Energy in transacting the most important Affairs, and may contribute as much to the Happiness of the Subjects, as even Liberty itself....

The Laws ought to be so framed, as to secure the Safety of every Citizen as much as possible.

The Equality of the Citizens consists in this; that they should all be subject to the same Laws.

This Equality requires Institutions so well adapted, as to prevent the Rich from oppressing those who are not so wealthy as themselves, and converting all the Charges and Employments intrusted to them as Magistrates only, to their own private Emolument....

In a State or Assemblage of People that live together in a Community, where there are Laws, Liberty can only consist in doing that which every One ought to do, and not to be constrained to do that which One ought not to do.

A Man ought to form in his own Mind an exact and clear Idea of what Liberty is. Liberty is the Right of doing whatsoever the Laws allow: And if any one Citizen could do what the Laws forbid, there would be no more Liberty; because others would have an equal Power of doing the same.

The political Liberty of a Citizen is the Peace of Mind arising from the Consciousness, that every Individual enjoys his peculiar Safety; and in order that the People might attain this Liberty, the Laws ought to be so framed, that no one Citizen should stand in Fear of another; but that all of them should stand in Fear of the same Laws....

The Usage of Torture is contrary to all the Dictates of Nature and Reason; even Mankind itself cries out against it, and demands loudly the total Abolition of it.

That Law, therefore, is highly beneficial to the Community where it is established, which ordains that every Man shall be judged by his Peers and Equals. For when the Fate of a Citizen is in Question, all Prejudices arising from the Difference of Rank or Fortune should be stifled; because they ought to have no Influence between the Judges and the Parties accused.

No Man ought to be looked upon as guilty, before he has received his judicial Sentence; nor can the Laws deprive him of their Protection, before it is proved that he has forfeited all Right to it. What Right therefore can Power give to any to inflict Punishment upon a Citizen at a Time, when it is yet dubious, whether he is Innocent or guilty?

A Society of Citizens, as well as every Thing else, requires a certain fixed Order: There ought to be some to govern, and others to obey. And this is the Origin of every Kind of Subjection; which feels itself more or less alleviated, in Proportion to the Situation of the Subjects. And, consequently, as the Law of Nature commands Us to take as much Care, as lies in Our Power, of the Prosperity of all the People; we are obliged to alleviate the Situation of the Subjects, as much as sound Reason will permit. And therefore, to shun all Occasions of reducing People to a State of Slavery, except the utmost Necessity should inevitably oblige us to do it; in that Case, it ought not to be done for our own Benefit; but for the Interest of the State: Yet even that Case is extremely uncommon. Of whatever Kind Subjection may be, the civil Laws ought to guard, on the one Hand, against the Abuse of Slavery, and, on the other, against the Dangers which may arise from it.

It seems too, that the Method of exacting their Revenues, newly invented by the Lords, diminishes both the Inhabitants, and the Spirit of Agriculture in Russia. Almost all the Villages are heavily taxed. The Lords, who seldom or never reside in their Villages, lay an Impost on every Head of one, two, and even five Rubles, without the least Regard to the Means by which their Peasants may be able to raise this Money.

It is highly necessary that the Law should prescribe a Rule to the Lords, for a more judicious Method of raising their Revenues; and oblige them to levy such a Tax, as tends least to separate the Peasant from his House and Family; this would be the Means by which Agriculture would become more extensive, and Population be more increased in the Empire."

Still, Catherine was like any other 18th century monarchs in other respects, particularly when it came to expanding her empire. Poland, traditionally weak, was an easy acquisition, and since King Augustus III of Poland was dying without an heir. Catherine agreed to an alliance with Frederick II of Prussia to place her former lover, Stanislaus Poniatowski, on the Polish throne to succeed him. For some time after he left Russia, Catherine had remained emotionally tied to him, avoiding telling him of her involvement with Gregory Orlov or the birth of her third child. At the time Catherine became Empress, she still viewed Poniatowski as a powerful ally on the Polish throne. He was poor, would rely upon her for money and would remain loyal because he loved her. In short, he was little more than a political pawn. While she was not a fan of Frederick, these two great powers could together easily pressure the Polish nobility.

Catherine again intervened in Polish affairs two years later. Hoping to appease the Orthodox Church, she required increased religious tolerance in Poland. When Polish Catholics objected, causing significant unrest, she sent Russian troops into Poland, sparking a war with Turkey. While they were allies, as long as Catherine faced only a single enemy, Prussia was not required, by treaty, to respond. Frederick feared that the war might grow and sought a diplomatic solution, dividing more than a third of Poland between Prussia, Russia and Austria. The war with Turkey continued until 1774, when it ended with the Treaty of Kuchak Kainardzhi. By this time, Catherine had made substantial gains, particularly along the Black Sea. Turkey agreed to pay a substantial war indemnity and Catherine gained the right to trade freely in the seas under Turkish control.

Unfortunately, the peace was short lived. The second Turkish war began with a sudden declaration of war by the Turkish sultan in 1787, and Sweden also seized upon the opportunity, declaring war in 1788. However, Sweden lacked the forces necessary to succeed, and when the King of Sweden made astonishing demands, Catherine simply had to maintain the status quo in Finland. By the summer of 1790, the short-lived war with Sweden was over.

Meanwhile, Catherine still had to deal with Turkey. Austria was, by treaty, committed to the defense of Russia and Gregory Potemkin, now the head of the army, led the military response. The war continued with significant losses on both sides until the death of Joseph II, and after the war's conclusion, Austria signed an armistice with the Ottoman Empire. Peace between Russia and Turkey followed in the summer of 1791.

Chapter 6: Catherine the Mother of Russia

"Assuredly men of merit are never lacking at any time, for those are the men who manage affairs, and it is affairs that produce the men. I have never searched, and I have always found under my hand the men who have served me, and for the most part I have been well served." – Catherine the Great

The institution of serfdom began in late 16th century Russia to keep the serfs working the same plot of land, no matter who owned it. It also guaranteed them a number of rights and privileges that, over the next two centuries, were stripped away. Serfs could be bought and sold, families could be broken up without regard for their own well-being, and the serf lived or died as his or her owner chose.

By the time of Catherine's rule, approximately 1 million male serfs were under the control of the Church, half a million owned by the crown, 2.5 million by the state, and more than 5 million by the nobility. While most serfs were tied to land owned by the Church, state or nobility, others were the property of mines or foundries and had been since the time of Peter the Great. The lot of industrial serfs was significantly worse than that of those who farmed the land, as they worked in horrible conditions and their lives were short and harsh even by Russian standards. This state of affairs often led to riots.

Over a period of several years, Catherine, impacted by her own Enlightenment era studies on the natural rights of humans, considered the plight of these individuals. While she personally disapproved of the notion of serfdom, Catherine had little immediate recourse to end it. In 1767 she issued a decree regarding the nature of serfdom:

"The Governing Senate. . . has deemed it necessary to make known... that the landlords' serfs and peasants . . . owe their landlords proper submission and absolute obedience in all matters, according to the laws that have been enacted from time immemorial by the autocratic forefathers of Her Imperial Majesty and which have not been repealed, and which provide that all persons who dare to incite serfs and peasants to disobey their landlords shall be arrested and taken to the nearest government office, there to be punished forthwith as disturbers of the public tranquillity, according to the laws and without leniency. And should it so happen that even after the publication of the present decree of Her Imperial Majesty any serfs and peasants should cease to give the proper obedience to their landlords . . . and should make bold to submit unlawful petitions complaining of their landlords, and especially to petition Her Imperial Majesty personally, then both those who make the complaints and those who write up the petitions shall be punished by the knout and forthwith deported to Nerchinsk to penal servitude for life and shall be counted as part of the quota of recruits which their landlords must furnish to the army. And in order that people everywhere may know of the present decree, it shall be read in all the churches on Sundays and holy days for one month after it is received and therafter once every year during the great church festivals, lest anyone pretend ignorance."

As the tone of the decree suggests, serfs did not fare well under Catherine's reign, and she made no moves to improve the lives or conditions of either agricultural or industrial serfs. But she did tackle the question of their health and high infant mortality in part by establishing the first College of Medicine in Russia and recruiting doctors from throughout Europe to teach and work in Russia until native doctors could be trained. Each province was to have at least one hospital in its capital, and in Moscow there was also a specialized hospital dedicated to the treatment of sexually transmitted diseases. She also paid for a new lying-in and foundling hospital out of her personal income to reduce the rates of infanticide in Moscow. A system of baskets and bells allowed a mother to leave her newborn, without being seen, at a foundling hospital where conditions were good, with clean beds, ample food, and education. Children raised in the foundling hospital were guaranteed their freedom when grown and were given a vocational education to support themselves as urban citizens.

While Catherine herself rarely used the services of court doctors, the Russian state and Russian people still faced a serious threat. Smallpox killed without regard to social status or style of living, and in 1767 several members of the Austrian Hapsburg dynasty contracted smallpox, leading to multiple deaths. As a result, the Hapsburg empress Maria Theresa had her remaining children inoculated. At this time, inoculation required the injection of matter drawn from the pox of an individual with a mild, not overly serious, case of smallpox. It was still quite a new science and considered dangerous.

Fearing for the health of her son Paul, as well as her own well-being, Catherine invited Thomas Dimsdale, author of *The Present Method of Inoculating for the Small Pox*, to visit her court and explain his methods. She was vaccinated on October 12, 1768 and did not become seriously ill, merely developing a number of pox that healed within a week. She then had Paul inoculated, along with many of the Russian nobility. Inoculation clinics were soon established throughout Russia, and by 1780, more than 20,000 Russians had been inoculated against smallpox. Catherine's wisdom was confirmed when only a few years later smallpox took the life of the King of France, Louis XV.

While Catherine battled smallpox successfully, setting a valuable example for her people and promoting a life-saving inoculation, she could not fight another disease that would devastate Russia during her reign. Bubonic plague, known as the Black Death in fourteenth-century Europe, struck Russia in 1770, and spread throughout the country over the next year. Catherine initiated quarantine procedures in an attempt to stop the spread of plague, but by fall the death toll in Moscow was as high as 800 people per day. The city was in chaos and the governor of Moscow wrote Catherine asking permission to leave. Gregory Orlov assembled a team and went to Moscow personally to manage the epidemic, resulting in a dramatic drop in deaths over the next few months.

While Catherine viewed herself as an Enlightened monarch, literate, cultured and thoughtful, the people of western Europe viewed her very differently. She was believed to be guilty of Peter's murder and implicated in the murder of Ivan VI as well. Moreover, Russia was widely considered unenlightened and certainly not fashionable. Catherine attempted to begin a correspondence with the French writer and philosopher Voltaire not long after she ascended to the throne, but Voltaire was reluctant to start a relationship, believing her rule would be short-lived. Eventually Catherine's communications got through, and the two eventually began a regular correspondence that continued for many years. Catherine wrote to the famous satirist, "Your wit makes others witty."

Furthermore, Catherine developed a relationship with the philosopher (and eventual encyclopedia author) Denis Diderot. While Diderot was well-known, he had not been financially successful, but late in his life Catherine purchased his entire library on the condition that it remain with him throughout his life. She also provided him a generous salary to care for it. When his salary was not paid on time by the Russian government, Catherine sent him fifty times the amount owed. Diderot, who quite disliked traveling, eventually made the long journey to Russia, where he and Catherine spent two hours together in lively conversation each day. As Voltaire hoped Frederick II of Prussia would become his ideal ruler of the Enlightenment era, so Diderot believed that Catherine could be his. But when he realized Catherine, while happy to have intellectual discussions, would not implement any of his many suggestions, he left Russia. Catherine hinted at the difference between philosophy and actual rule in one letter to him, writing, "You philosophers are lucky men. You write on paper and paper is patient. Unfortunate Empress that I am, I write on the susceptible skins of living beings."

Diderot

Diderot was the only one of the prominent French intellectuals of the Enlightenment that Catherine met, but she developed a lasting and significant relationship with Friedrich Melchior Grimm. Grimm, editor of the *Correspondence Litteraire*, journeyed to St. Petersburg with Paul's bride, Princess Wilhelmina of Hesse-Darmstadt and arrived in St. Petersburg shortly before Diderot in 1773. Like Catherine, he was German by birth, and the two became quite close, with Catherine even sharing her personal thoughts about the state, politics, and even her lovers.

By 1773, Catherine had weathered war, smallpox and the bubonic plague, and that year she would face an internal rebellion known as the *Pugachevshcina*. Led by the Don Cossack Emalyan Pugachev, disenfranchised people moved against the government, coming from far from the cities of Russia, along the steppes and in the Ural mountains. The Cossack populations in these regions had long resented imperial interference and had, because of their isolated nature, been largely self-governing. But during the Turkish war, they were more frequently recruited to serve in the army and were expected to pay taxes more regularly. Catherine first learned of the rebellion in October 1773, when Emalyan Pugachev claimed to be the now-dead former emperor Peter III. While Pugachev did not physically resemble the tall, slender Peter III, Peter had reigned for a very short time and his image had not circulated, making Pugachev's ploy at least one worth trying. Pugachev described an assassination attempt made by Catherine against him due to her objections to his plan to free the serfs. He promised that he would, as ruler, free the serfs, allow people to worship in the old ways, and provide salt and other commodities free of charge to all Cossacks. He even created his own court, naming friends after the nobles in St. Petersburg, and dictated imperial decrees to his secretary.

Early in the rebellion, Catherine paid it little attention and sent only a small force, since most of the army was occupied in Turkey. The region was typically unstable, so she initially figured this was just another manifestation of a minor, ongoing difficulty. But meanwhile, Pugachev and his army moved through the land, killing the nobility and villagers who remained loyal to the Empress. Towns began to surrender to avoid being plundered, and in January 1774 Catherine resorted to labeling Pugachev a "common highway robber".

By the spring of 1774, Catherine realized the seriousness of the situation and that she was faced with a full-blown rebellion. With much of the army still in Turkey, she created a loyal volunteer force that succeeded in breaking up Pugachev's army, but Pugachev escaped into the Ural mountains and remained in hiding for several months before reappearing with an army of 20,000 men in July of 1774, destroying much of the city of Kazan. The Russian army responded forcefully and successfully, forcing Pugachev to flee to the south as his men began to desert him. Forces under the command of Peter Panin followed Pugachev and his remaining troops, and by August the people along the Volga River were denouncing Pugachev as an imposter. He was defeated for the last time on August 24, but escaped by swimming across the Volga River. Panin finally captured him on September 30, 1774 and brought him before the empress that November. He was interrogated for six weeks, and eventually beheaded, drawn and quartered. Catherine issued a broad pardon thereafter, but many of her nobles responded violently against those who had rebelled. This impressed Catherine, and she kept in mind throughout the remainder of her reign that the nobles had supported her while the people had opposed her.

Chapter 7: Catherine the Matriarch

Catherine remained loyal and faithful to Gregory Orlov until 1772, when he shamed himself in the peace talks with the Turks. She decided to end the relationship and had a brief affair with a young man in the court, Alexander Vasilchikov, and when Orlov returned to St. Petersburg he found that Vasilchikov had taken his place. However, Vasilchikov, while attractive, soon bored Catherine, and in 1774 she began an affair with Gregory Potemkin. Potemkin was from a poor but noble family, and he was intelligent, thoughtful and well-spoken. After beginning his studies in the University of Moscow, he joined the army, and after his romantic gesture on the march to Peterhof, he was welcomed at court and frequently invited to social gatherings. He gained rank and served loyally for a number of years. Late in 1773, Catherine invited him to write to her privately, and the two engaged in a back-and-forth flirtation for some time before beginning a relationship in February 1774.

Potemkin

At once, the vainglorious Potemkin began to define his own rank in the court, aided by the fact that the two were passionately in love. Even today love notes between the two survive, often written and delivered from room to room in the palace. They spent several hours together each night, their apartments linked by a private stairway, and they may have married privately in 1774. Beginning in the late spring of 1774, Catherine privately addressed him as "my husband" and "my spouse". Their relationship continued for the rest of Potemkin's life, even after each would take other lovers.

Along with love came a sharing of power, and Potemkin took an active role in running the government from 1774 onward. In 1776, at Catherine's request, the Austrian emperor made Potemkin a prince of the Holy Roman Empire, and in the years that followed he gained control of much of southern Russia and improved conditions there. He took Catherine on a tour of these lands in 1787, revealing clean, newly built villages, vineyards and fields, but it was widely rumored that these were a pretense only meant to impress the Empress by hiding the unsavory state of things. In fact, the rumors took such strong hold that Potemkin is best remembered today for lending his name to the phrase "Potemkin Village", which describes something that superficially looks good in order to deceive viewers of the bare reality contained within. If it was a ruse, however, it fooled more than Catherine; contemporaries, including several ambassadors, shared similar descriptions of the positive conditions in southern Russia under Potemkin's supervision. On the same journey, Catherine met with Stanislaus Poniatowski, King of Poland, and Joseph II, Emperor of Austria.

While she still cared deeply for Potemkin, over the ensuing years their passion began to fade and Catherine started looking elsewhere. She began, with Potemkin's knowledge, a relationship with Peter Zavadovsky, who remained her favorite for only 18 months, and Catherine had a number of later lovers, but none served a political function. These men were chosen from her guard, enjoyed her favor and were quickly replaced. While the courts of Europe widely accepted affairs, Catherine's willingness to choose young men to entertain her was considered scandalous. Still, none took Potemkin's place, and when he became ill in the fall of 1791, Catherine was quite concerned. She was completely devastated when he died in October 1791.

Catherine had two living children but only acknowledged her son Paul as her heir, and she was careful to define him as her heir rather than Peter's to avoid any questions of paternity. Paul, who resembled Peter somewhat, was often ill, so it was decided that he should marry and hopefully father a child, just in case he died young. Catherine offered him the choice of three German princesses, sisters from Hesse-Darmstadt, and he chose Wilhelmina. As Elizabeth had done with Catherine so many years earlier, Catherine had Wilhelmina converted to Russian Orthodox and gave her the name Natalia. Paul and Natalia married on September 29, 1773.

Unfortunately, Natalia and Catherine had other similarities. Natalia was apparently unimpressed by Paul and spent too lavishly for Catherine's liking. Catherine often criticized her daughter in law until 1775, when Natalia became pregnant. The court prepared for the birth in 1776, but while the pregnancy went smoothly, her labor continued for five day before Natalia succumbed to the pain and blood loss. The male baby died with her. Catherine and Paul had remained with Natalia through the birth and were devastated by the loss, but Catherine eventually grew so tired of Paul's ongoing grief that she presented him with evidence of his wife's affair before her pregnancy. The Empress was much more bothered by the loss of a healthy male child and the burden of having to find a new bride for Paul.

With the support of Frederick of Prussia, Catherine chose Princess Sophia of Wittenburg as Paul's second wife. Now 17, the girl was already engaged, but that engagement was easily broken. Sophia was attractive, modest and good-natured. Paul traveled to Berlin to meet his future bride, and the fact that he was already enamored with all things German ensured that the trip improved the young widower's mood significantly. In September, Sophia, now called Maria, arrived in Russia, and she was quickly converted and betrothed. The two were married on September 26, 1776 and Maria delivered a healthy son, Alexander, only 14 months later. A second boy, Constantine, followed 18 months after, as did others, for a total of nine healthy children. Catherine took a significant role in the raising of Paul's first two sons, choosing their nurses, tutors and eventually wives. Paul and Maria were allowed to raise their five daughters and third son, born the year of Catherine's death.

Paul and Maria were happy together and it was a good match. In 1781, they toured Western Europe together, and when they visited Paris they were welcomed by Marie Antoinette and Louis XVI. But upon their return, Catherine criticized both of them, and Paul found that his beloved tutor, Panin, was dying. He soon learned that he would not be allowed to serve in the army or wield political power of any sort and became frustrated, often lashing out against those around him. Bereft of any important duties, Paul created a small private force of soldiers and put them through Prussian style drills, not unlike Peter III.

Paul was especially bothered by the role played by his mother's favorites and lovers in court. While he could have been crowned her co-ruler, Catherine viewed her son as competition rather than a potential asset. Over time, Paul became progressively more unbalanced until even his wife acknowledged that he was unwell. Catherine almost certainly considered naming Alexander her heir, bypassing Paul altogether, but if she produced a will to this effect it was ultimately destroyed rather than acknowledged.

In 1796, Catherine, at 67, was still lively and devoted to her work. On November 5, she rose as usual, but as she worked alone in her rooms she suffered a stroke. Paul and Maria, as well as others in the court, surrounded the dying Empress, and when the doctors told him she would not regain consciousness Paul ordered paperwork drawn up for his accession to the throne. Catherine the Great died on the night of November 6, 1796, and Paul had her buried together with the exhumed body of Peter III in the Cathedral of St. Peter and Paul, near the grave of Peter the Great. In her will, she requested, "Lay out my corpse dressed in white, with a golden crown on my head, and on it inscribe my Christian name. Mourning dress is to be worn for six months, and no longer: the shorter the better." Her wishes were fulfilled.

Chapter 8: Legacy

Catherine the Great had ruled for the better part of three decades, and she oversaw a considerable transformation of Russia during her reign, but Russia was still considered "other" by the Western Europeans, no matter how hard Catherine tried to cultivate the Enlightenment and claim it for herself and her people. For that reason, a general lack of information and the spread of rumors and scandalous information about Catherine led to an even more colorful and far more controversial legacy than the politically cunning, strong-willed Empress deserved.

Perhaps the most famous legends about Catherine surround how she died, the most persistent being that she died while attempting to have intercourse with a horse. The story is patently untrue, despite still being common today, and it was almost certainly inspired by the fact that Catherine's contemporaries considered her sexual proclivities to be voracious based on the fact that she continued taking on new, young lovers well into her twilight years. In his epic poem *Don Juan*, Lord Byron's famous title character becomes one of Catherine's lovers when he's just 22 years old. In truth, when it came to her sexual activities, Catherine's behavior was so typical among monarchs of the period that it almost certainly received mention among her contemporaries only due to the fact she was a woman.

Another legend made reference to the fact she suffered a stroke in her bathroom, which got turned into her dying on the toilet (similar to the Elvis legend). Renowned Russian author Aleksandr Pushkin made a pun out of this story in an untitled poem, literally writing of Catherine in verse, "Decreed the orders, burned the fleets / And died boarding a vessel". But in Russian, the last line could also be translated as "And died sitting down on the toilet".

Indeed, the Western Europeans missed the forest for the trees, as Catherine was truly a remarkable and influential ruler. She modernized Russia from the inside, pulling in Enlightened ideals and overseeing the construction of new towns, her law code was progressive for the times, and her empire expanded in all directions, from Poland to Alaska. She admired Peter the Great, and in the end she emulated him, making it no surprise that Russians continue to look back fondly on Catherine and her reign as a Golden Age.

Bibliography

Massie, Robert. Catherine the Great: Portrait of a Woman. New York, NY: Random House, 2012

Rounding, Virginia. Catherine the Great: Love, Sex and Power. New York, NY: St. Martin's Griffin, 2008.

Printed in Great Britain
by Amazon.co.uk, Ltd.,
Marston Gate.